Hong Kong

120th anniversary
Berlitz

- A 👉 in the text denotes a highly recommended sight
- A complete A–Z of practical information starts on p.102
- Mapping on cover flaps

Berlitz Publishing Company, Inc.

Princeton   Mexico City   Dublin   Eschborn   Singapore

Text:	Ken Bernstein
Editors:	Hazel Clarke, Clare Haigh
Photography:	Chris Coe, Walter Imber
Layout:	Media Content Marketing, Inc.
Cartography:	🌀 Falk-Verlag, Munich

Thanks to Alex Leung, Kindy Lam, Caitlin West, Londy Chan, Kwondy Ying-wai, Li Musheng, and Kenneth Newport for their help in updating this guide.

Found an error we should know about? Our editor would be happy to hear from you, and a postcard would do. Although we make every effort to ensure the accuracy of all the information in this book, changes do occur.

ISBN 2-8315-6324-0
Revised 1998 – Second Printing May 1998

Printed in Switzerland by Weber SA, Bienne
029/805 RP

CONTENTS

HONG KONG

THE REGION AND
ITS PEOPLE

Exciting, mysterious, glamorous, clamorous — these words have described Hong Kong for at least a century. And, yes, they still pertain after the momentous events of July 1, 1997, when the former British colony became a special administrative region of the People's Republic of China. In fact, once news of the handover vanished from the front pages of newspapers, the two main topics of conversation once again took prominence, as they have for decades — the economy and housing (of which there never seems to be enough to accommodate an almost steady influx of new residents).

When you visit Hong Kong today your impressions will be the same as they would have been if you'd been here before the handover — frenetic commerce and millions of people.

The people of Hong Kong — almost 98 percent are Chinese — are packed into the skyscrapers and double-decker trams. To get away from it all, take a bus to the hinterland, where water buffalo still do the drudgery, or sail to one of the nearby deserted islands.

Hong Kong ("Fragrant Harbour"), the best known of the former territory's 235 islands, contains a quarter of the total population. Yet it accounts for only a small fraction of the real estate, most of which is on the mainland in the so-called New Territories. The British leased this land from China at the end of the 19th century. The contract expired at midnight, 30 June, 1997.

Initially, Hong Kong's role was simply that of a trading post; now, the economy has moved into the booming realm of manufacturing and exports. Local factories sell textiles, clothing, toys, electronics, and plastics to the world. The work force enjoys Asia's third-highest take-home wages (after Japan and Singapore), and is highly motivated. So are the bosses, who pay only a 16.5 percent business profits tax.

The *laissez-faire* economic scene attracts investors from all sides, not least from the rest of China itself. Hong Kong has long been China's handiest window on the West. This is only one of the reasons behind Beijing's announced determination to maintain Hong Kong's prosperity and stability.

According to a 1984 agreement between the Chinese and the British governments, Hong Kong has remained a capitalist enclave after the People's Republic took control in 1997, and the Hong Kong dollar — which is the currency of the world's biggest financial centre — remains freely convertible. The 1984 agreement guaranteed the people representative government, continued free speech, and travel, and justice based on British law. At the time of the takeover the new government assured the people that their laws and rights

---

A Kowtow to Chinese

Chinese, the world's most spoken language, has also recorded the history and culture of a nation for thousands of years.

Each character represents an idea, not a sound, and the way it's written is also important, as the Chinese consider calligraphy a serious art form. Writing a single character requires from 1 to 33 pen or brush strokes. Chinese can be written from left to right, top to bottom, or — in some cases — right to left.

The spoken language has additional challenges. The dialects in various regions can be as different as English and French. The Cantonese spoken in Hong Kong is difficult for foreigners because it uses up to seven different musical inflections — "tones" — to distinguish otherwise identical syllables.

Aberdeen's large "floating population" lives aboard houseboats like this one.

would remain unchanged. Many people are dubious but at the same time they can't see Hong Kong being anything other than a capitalist enclave.

The territory's exact area is flexible, growing slightly from year to year as more land is reclaimed from the sea. It is just over 1,095 square km (423 square miles) in total — about the same size as Tahiti, Martinique, or the Orkneys. However, there are about 6½ million people crammed into the islands, and the population density is duly noted in the record books.

Thanks to the subtropical climate, the people can escape from their sardine-can living quarters into the streets. Hence you will see a round-the-clock outdoor drama played out by the bargain-hawkers, noodle-vendors, hair-cutters, fortune-tellers, and story-tellers.

Tens of thousands beat the housing problem as part of the floating population, and the term can be taken quite literally: they live on junks in harbours and in typhoon shelters, which may house three or four generations. Thousands more live in shack communities. At the other extreme are the millionaires with conspicuous luxuries such as their ocean-view mansions and lucky-number license plates (which cost a fortune at government auctions) on their limousines.

Hong Kong has many hundreds of Christian churches and chapels, but most people follow Buddhism, Taoism, or Confucianism. Holidays are eagerly observed. In temples crammed into narrow streets or in monasteries aloof in the wilderness, a multitude of gods are worshiped.

Fate and luck are taken very seriously in Hong Kong. The astrologers and fortune-tellers do a steady business. Even before a skyscraper can be built, for example, a *fung shui* (wind and water) investigation approves its site, and the spirits must be placated. Gambling is a passion, whether cards, mah-jong, the lottery, or the horses. Hong Kong has two major race tracks as well as an intensive off-track betting system.

The people of Hong Kong are good at numbers; watch an abacus in a race against an electronic calculator. They're also

Children are schooled in both Chinese and English in Hong Kong's crowded classrooms.

Small and simple boats on the harbor contrast the enormous scale of Hong Kong's skyline.

good at letters, including the 26 of the English language. Even in an isolated village you'll find someone who can muster up a few words of English. The population is highly literate: more than 60 Chinese-language newspapers are published in Hong Kong as well as two English dailies. Although the official language is now Mandarin, most people in Hong Kong speak Cantonese, a dialect unintelligible to natives of Beijing or Shanghai.

> Although there are numerous Chinese dialects, the written language is everywhere the same and is understood by all.

Sightseeing in Hong Kong starts at sea level with a harbour as those at San Francisco and Rio de Janeiro. The water traffic is enthralling — a bubbling cosmopolitan stew of freighters, ferries, tugs, junks, sampans, and yachts. Try seeing it from a ferryboat weaving through the nautical throng, or look down on it from Victoria Peak. At 548 metres (1,800 feet), the Peak is a modest mountain, but it's the island's summit in both altitude and social standing.

Elsewhere on the island, there are sights to match every interest and mood. One minute you can be serious among skyscrapers in this great centre of finance, and the next you're escaping to Aw Boon Haw Gardens, an Asian ancestor of Disneyland, or visiting Ocean Park to look at the fish and the birds. Curiosity, or an appetite for seafood, might lead you to Aberdeen, one of the liveliest fishing harbours you have ever seen, and you'll need no excuse to investigate the dozen principal beaches.

Across Victoria Harbour is the mainland, starting in the overcrowded Kowloon peninsula with its hotels, nightlife, and almost non-stop shopping. Beyond, in the New Territories, the colony changes character from mile to mile: here a brand-new suburb, there an industrial complex, and beyond that a wilderness of fish ponds, duck farms, and banana plantations. Near the frontier, the terrain becomes as pastoral as the China depicted in old watercolours. You can climb to the lookout point at Lok Ma Chau and peer out over the mainland.

Busy nightclubs, restaurants, hotels and shops line Kowloon's colorful Nathan Road.

You don't just have to be satisfied with a glance through binoculars. The Beijing government is allowing access to foreign tourists in ever more significant numbers, and Hong Kong is the principal gateway.

The most popular getaway spot for the people of Hong Kong is the enclave of Macau, less than an hour's ride by jet-foil. The 400-year-old blend of Iberian and Asian cultures makes Macau, a Portuguese colony until it becomes independent in 1999, a fascinating place, full of old colonial grace and boundless contemporary energy and ingenuity. With its cobbled streets and sandy beaches, Macau can be calm and restful. On the other side of the coin, it is a revel of roulette, blackjack, fan-tan, dog-racing, horse-racing, and jai-alai.

Back in Hong Kong, you'll need some time and strength — and money — for shopping. The range of goods is exciting. But to find exactly what you want at the best price will require some concentrated window shopping. The bargains may be as old as traditional Chinese porcelain or as new as the latest camcorders and electronic equipment.

Hong Kong also excels in food. You'll never be disappointed, whether you're pampered in one of the top luxury restaurants or just munching a morsel bought from a push-cart. This is the place to try every kind of Chinese cooking, not only the familiar Cantonese, but specialities from the lesser-known gastronomic regions. Hong Kong also offers a wide variety of European-style restaurants; even hamburger joints and pizza parlours.

Nightlife is not as one-sided as you may have been led to believe. Yes, there are a thousand Suzie Wongs in Wanchai and Tsim Sha Tsui, but Hong Kong also has sophisticated cabarets, arts festivals, and its own philharmonic orchestra.

The wail of Chinese opera, the clang of a tram, the chant of a peddler, the clatter of mah-jong tiles: Hong Kong is never still. It's as dynamic, and unpredictable, as a typhoon.

A BRIEF HISTORY

Accounts of Hong Kong's history often begin in the year 1841, though the territory had been populated for several thousands of years before the British set foot on it. Fishermen were the first settlers on Lamma and Lantau islands. Later, during Europe's Middle Ages, the port of Shek Pai Wan (now called Aberdeen) flourished as a pirates' lair. In the New Territories, Chinese settlers lived in small, traditional walled villages. Lord Palmerston, in the mid-19th century, dismissed Hong Kong as "a barren island with hardly a house upon it." The Foreign Secretary believed the place had no future—he couldn't have been more mistaken.

The China Trade

Long before the days of Lord Palmerston, the British East India Company had a thriving business in Canton, buying Chinese tea, silk, and porcelain for an insatiable English market. But the trading conditions were difficult. The emperor considered his country to be both self-sufficient and superior. He also kept the traders in a confined area to minimize the harmful influence of the "foreign devils" on the population in general.

For the British, the problem was not so much one of dignity as of balancing the books. China would accept nothing but silver bullion in exchange for its goods. Britain had to look for a more abundant commodity to square the accounts —something other than silver to fill the holds of the clipper ships on the way to the East.

Around the turn of the 19th century the traders found the answer: opium. They loaded it in India and delivered it to Canton. China outlawed the trade in 1799, but local Can-

Historical Landmarks

1799	China outlaws opium trade.
1840	First Opium War
1841	Hong Kong handed over to Britain in peace agreement.
1842	Further Opium War results in Treaty of Nanking; China opens five ports to foreign penetration. Hong Kong confirmed as free port.
1860	Britain wins Kowloon peninsula.
1898	By Convention of Peking, China leases New Territories and 235 islands to Britain for 99 years.
1911	Manchu Dynasty overthrown in Chinese revolutions; thousands seek refuge in Hong Kong.
1931	Japan invades China; more refugees arrive.
1941	Japan attacks Pearl Harbour (Dec. 7). Hong Kong surrenders to Japan (Dec. 25).
1940s	Population reduced by deportation of Chinese to the mainland by occupying Japanese forces.
Post-war	Massive influx of Chinese refugees from mainland civil war, resulting in housing problems by 1950.
1953	Fire destroys squatters' city in Kowloon; government launches emergency housing programme.
1962	Borders closed to Chinese refugees.
1981	Nationality Act assigns British Dependent Territories Citizenship to people of Hong Kong.
1989	Tiananmen Square Massacre increases concern for the future of Hong Kong under Chinese rule.
1990	Final text of Basic Law set out by China outlining rule after 1997. Brain drain continues.
1997	On June 30 Hong Kong reverts to Chinese rule as a *"special administrative region."*

tonese officials were always willing to look the other way for a consideration—"squeeze money," as it is still known in Hong Kong. The traffic in opium became so intense that China found its silver surplus beginning to melt away.

The Manchu emperor eventually laid down the law in 1839. He commanded Commissioner Lin Tse-hsu to go to Canton and stamp out the smuggling of "foreign mud," as the Chinese called opium. Bribable bureaucrats panicked at Lin's appointment; his incorruptibility was notorious. Lin's crackdown was indeed severe. He demanded that the British merchants in Canton surrender their opium stores. To back up the ultimatum he laid siege to the traders, who were confined to their Canton quarters. After six tense weeks the top British official on the scene, Captain Charles Elliot, promised the merchants compensation if they would obey Lin. They surrendered over 20,000 chests of opium to the commissioner and retreated to temporary sanctuary, first in Macau, and later on ships anchored in Hong Kong harbour.

A year later, in June 1840, a British naval force was dispatched to retaliate against the Chinese, thus beginning the first of the so-called Opium Wars. After a few skirmishes and much negotiation, a peace agreement was reached. Under the Convention of Chuenpi, Britain was given the island of Hong Kong, and on 26 January, 1841, Elliot proclaimed it a British colony.

Opium War II

The peace plan achieved at Chuenpi was short-lived. Both Peking and London repudiated the agreement and fighting resumed. This time the British forces, less than 3,000 strong but in possession of superior weapons and tactics, did outfight the Chinese. Shanghai fell and Nanking was threatened, so the Manchus were forced back to the negotiating table. In the Treaty of Nanking (1842) China was compelled to open five of its ports to foreign economic and political penetration, and even to compensate the opium smugglers for their losses. Hong Kong's status as a British colony and a free port was confirmed.

In the aftermath of the Opium Wars the trade in "foreign mud" was resumed at a level even higher than before, although the major traders, by now respectable and diversified, stopped their trading in 1907. The British didn't abolish opium smoking in Hong Kong until 1946; in China the new Communist government followed suit in 1949.

Craftsmanship from China's history—now to be found in Hong Kong's antique shops.

Thriving Colony

The man who won the Opium War and the peace that followed, Sir Henry Pottinger, became the first governor of Hong Kong. Under his direction the colony began its march toward what he predicted would be "a vast emporium of commerce and wealth."

And he was right. Almost as soon as the Union Jack was hoisted, Hong Kong's population and economy began to grow steadily. One surprise was the sizeable number of Chinese who

*Standing guard over Macau
—once the gateway
to China.*

chose to move to the colony. One early governor, Sir John Francis Davis, fed up with the squabbling of the English residents, said, "It is a much easier task to govern the 20,000 Chinese inhabitants of the colony than the few hundreds of English."

Despite the differences between the Chinese majority and the European minority, relations were generally cordial except for one rare incident. On 15 January, 1857, somebody added an extra ingredient to the dough at the colony's main bakery: arsenic. While the Chinese continued to enjoy their daily rice, the occidentals, eating their daily bread, were dropping like flies. At the height of the panic engendered by the poison plot, thousands of Chinese were deported from Hong Kong, though no one ever discovered the identity or the motives of the culprit or plotters.

By a treaty in 1860, Britain gained a permanent beachhead on the Chinese mainland—the Kowloon peninsula, directly across Victoria harbour from Hong Kong island. In 1898, under the Convention of Peking, China leased the New Territories and 235 more islands to Britain for what then seemed an eternity—99 years.

Twentieth Century

The colony's population fluctuated according to events beyond its borders. In 1911, when the Chinese revolution overthrew the ruling Manchu Dynasty, refugees flocked to the safety of Hong Kong. Hundreds of thousands more arrived in the 1930s when Japan invaded China. By the eve of World War II, the population was more than 1½ million, far more than could be housed.

A few hours after Japan's attack on the American fleet at Pearl Harbor in December 1941, a dozen Japanese battalions began an assault on Hong Kong. The colony's woefully inadequate defenses were unprepared for such an attack. Five minutes of bombing destroyed Hong Kong's minimal air force on the airfield at Kai Tak. Abandoning the New Territories and Kowloon, the defenders retreated to Hong Kong island, hoping for relief which never came. They finally surrendered on Christmas Day in 1941. Veterans recall a subsequent three and a half cruel years of hunger during a concentration camp existence. The occupation forces deported many Hong Kong Chinese to the mainland, so the population was down to half a million by the time of Japan's defeat in 1945. At the end of World War II, Hong Kong took stock of what remained—no industry, no fishing fleet, and few houses and public services.

Typhoon

No natural danger poses more of a threat to Hong Kong than a typhoon, though with modern techniques of surveillance and early warning, precautions can be taken. Nevertheless, these tropical cyclones, with winds of 120 km (75 miles) and more per hour, cause casualties and damage almost every year.

Postwar Growth

China's civil war sent distressing echoes to Hong Kong. While the Chinese Communist armies gained the upper hand over the Nationalists and then drove towards the south, the flow of refugees into Hong Kong multiplied. Soon after Canton fell and the People's Republic was proclaimed, the total population of Hong Kong (1950) stood at two million people. Housing was in desperately short supply.

The problem became an outright disaster on Christmas Day 1953. An uncontrollable fire devoured a whole city of squatters' shacks in Kowloon; 50,000 refugees were deprived of even primitive shelter. The calamity spurred the government to launch an emergency programme of public-housing construction. The spartan new blocks of flats, grimly overcrowded, soon put cheap and fireproof roofs over hundreds of thousands of heads.

But even a frenzy of construction work couldn't keep pace with the demand for living space. Refugees continued to flee from China, legally and illegally, until 1962, when the colonial authorities closed the border. Next came the flood of boat people from Vietnam.

Into the Next Century

The tide began to turn, however, after the 1984 Joint Declaration was signed, in which Britain confirmed the handover of the New Territories and Hong Kong to China in 1997, while China promised that existing laws and civil liberties would be upheld. The British Nationality Act (1981) in effect prevented Hong Kong citizens from acquiring British citizenship, and thousands of people, anxious about their future under Chinese rule, were prompted to apply for citizenship elsewhere, notably in Canada and Australia.

Victoria Peak provides an impressive view of Hong Kong's tangle of towers and the harbour beyond.

Democracy protests in 1989 in Beijing's Tiananmen Square sparked off sympathy marches in Hong Kong, and further increased tension with China. In 1990 China issued its Basic Law, or mini-constitution for 1997, which included a clause stating that martial law would be imposed following any turmoil in the territory. Fears about the future of democracy increased, the numbers emigrating continued to rise, and companies moved their headquarters out of Hong Kong and beyond Beijing's reach.

Since the handover in July 1997, what has controlled heartbeats in Hong Kong are the fluctuations of the Hang Seng Index, foreign currency exchange rates, and property prices. In short, the status quo prevails. Everybody hopes Hong Kong will remain stable, but everyone also has their doubts that it will. In the meantime, the philosophy is to seize present-day opportunities, which boils down to making money in the thriving economy. And (as always) whatever its future, Hong Kong bristles with energy and ambition.

WHERE TO GO

Hong Kong International Airport and most of the hotels are in Kowloon, which is on the mainland side of the territory. The crowded Kowloon peninsula and the booming, but often bucolic, New Territories call for some serious sightseeing. But, for orientation, we begin across Victoria Harbour on Hong Kong island, where the colony was founded. The island remains the capital of government and of commerce, and presents a compact cross-section of all the territory's delights and pungent contrasts.

HONG KONG CENTRAL

No matter how many tunnels and transit systems may speed cross-harbour traffic, nothing matches the excitement of the **Star Ferry** between Kowloon and Hong Kong. Bells ring, deckhands in blue sailor suits man the hawsers, and a couple of hundred commuters begin an eight-minute adventure. As the big green-and-white boat weaves its way through an ever-changing obstacle course of both large and small craft, the soaring **skyline** of Hong Kong Central draws closer. If the captain fails to make a neat three-point landing, commuter passengers mill about impatiently, waiting for the gangplank to bang down, so that they can rush ashore. (Travellers in a hurry know that second-class, on the bottom deck, not only costs less but is faster, with fewer steps from ship to street.)

Once outside the terminal, tourists are solicited by rickshaw drivers as ancient as their vehicles. In the old days these were the only means of travel, but now they are mainly for tourist trips and photo opportunities. If your conscience, however, prevents you from taking a ride, you can settle for a posed photograph in the passenger seat. The driver, always ready to smile for a camera, will demand a model's fee.

Hong Kong Highlights

Aberdeen — Hong Kong island, South, (*Bus 7 or 70 from Central bus terminal*); at night, floating restaurants in Shum Wan harbour offer succulent seafood and a unique atmosphere. (See page 34)

Hollywood Road — Hong Kong island, Central; beautiful porcelain, rosewood furniture, carpets, and chinoiserie on offer in Hong Kong's antiques centre. (See page 30)

Jade Market — Kowloon (Yau Ma Tei MTR); market stalls devoted entirely to jade; visit early to avoid the afternoon crush. (See page 40)

Kat Hing Wai walled village — New Territories (*Tsuen Wan ferry from Sheung Wan, Bus 51*); narrow streets and stone houses in a 17th-century settlement in the village of Kam Tin. (See page 42)

Lei Cheng Uk Han Tomb — Sham Shui Po, Kowloon (Bus 2 from Star Ferry); this burial vault revealed a number of bronze and pottery objects, believed to date back to a.d. 25–220. (See page 39)

Po Lin Monastery — Lantau Island (Ferry from Central, Bus 2 from Mui Wo); one of the world's largest outdoor bronze statues of Buddha in the grounds of a monastery. (See page 47)

Stanley Market — Hong Kong island, South (Bus 6 or 260 from Central bus terminal); lively outdoor markets and bargain buys in a pretty fishing village. (See page 36)

Sung Dynasty Village — Lai Chi Kok, Kowloon (Mei Foo MTR); Reconstruction of Chinese community 1,000 years ago. (See page 41)

Tai O Fishing Village — Lantau Island (Bus 1 from Mui Wo); distinctive houses built on stilts above the river character. (See page 46)

Victoria Peak — Hong Kong island (accessible by Peak Tram); superb views over Hong Kong and the islands. (See page 26)

Some excellent free maps and brochures are available at a branch of the Hong Kong Tourist Association, situated at Shop 8, Basement, Jardine House. Brightly uniformed specialists are on hand to answer your questions in any of several languages. The 52-storey building, with porthole-shaped windows, certainly catches the eye.

There are no words in Chinese for *yes* and *no*. The sentence is repeated in the affirmative or negative (e.g. **Q:** Do you have…? – **A:** I have…/ I don't have…).

But the newer skyscrapers outdo this 1970s model in both altitude and panache. Just to the west of Jardine House is Exchange Square, a 52-storey complex encompassing a luxurious shopping mall. Inland, the Hong Kong Bank building (by architect Norman Foster) has a functional steel superstructure and a vast atrium. It is probably one of the most expensive structures ever built. At 72 storeys, the rival Bank of China building, which is owned by the People's Republic, was once known as the tallest building to be found outside North America. Its daringly eccentric design was created by I. M. Pei.

Most of the island's flashy skyscrapers have been built on the site of older colonial buildings, demolished in the path of progress. In spite of spirited attempts by preservationists, there is little that can be done to spare these landmarks, so severe is the shortage of suitable land. The government required payment of huge sums in compensation for the bulldozing of colonial glories, but the few remaining century-old structures — even the Anglican Cathedral — now crouch under the threat of destruction.

In Hong Kong, **City Hall** is not the place to look for politicians or bureaucrats. They're dispersed in office buildings in various parts of town. City Hall is, in fact, a modern cultural centre which occupies 9,300 square metres (100,000 square feet) of harbour-side land just east of Star Ferry. Its many facilities include the Hong Kong Museum of Art (see page 39), a library, and a 1,500-seat concert hall.

At times the whole district, except for Statue Square and Chater Garden, seems to be one big building site. However tall the skyscraper under construction, the scaffolding surrounding it is always made of bamboo. It's much lighter than metal, and it works (though a typhoon can wreak havoc on a bamboo-shrouded construction site).

All the trams in Hong Kong pass along **Des Voeux Road**. So does most of the money, as you'll realize when you see the rows of financial institutions that line the road. Farther along, the road becomes Queensway, where at number 66 you'll find the Government Publication Centre located on the ground

Some of the world's tallest buildings tower above the busy crowds in central Hong Kong.

floor. Books on local history, economics, and sociology, as well as wall-sized maps and charts, can be purchased here.

To the Summit

For more than 90 years the most exhilarating way up to Victoria Peak has been by funicular. The **Peak Tram** starts its climb just across the street from the American Consulate in Garden Road and makes its way, sometimes at a startlingly

---

Hong Kong Glossary

Getting around is difficult when place-names are pronounced totally differently in English and Cantonese. Kowloon (which means Nine Dragons) is pronounced more or less the same in both languages, but other names can be a problem. To give you a head start, here are 15 troublemakers: in the first column, the customary English name, in the second column, the approximate Cantonese pronunciation. And if that fails, point to the Chinese characters in the third column.

Aberdeen	*Heung gong jai*	香港仔
Causeway Bay	*Tung lo wan*	銅鑼灣
Central district	*Jung wan*	中環
Cross Harbour Tunnel	*Hoi dai sui do*	海底隧道
Happy Valley	*Pau ma dei*	跑馬地
Mandarin Hotel	*Man wa jau dim*	文華酒店
Ocean Park	*Hoi yeung gung yuen*	海洋公園
The Peak	*San deng*	山頂
Peak Tram	*Lam che*	纜車
Peninsula Hotel	*Boon do jau dim*	半島酒店
Post office	*Yau jing guk*	郵政局
Railway station	*Fo che jam*	火車站
Repulse Bay	*Chin sui wan*	淺水灣
Stanley	*Chek chue*	赤柱
Star Ferry Pier	*Tin sing ma tau*	天星碼頭

steep incline, to the summit at 398 metres (1,305 feet). The right-of-way travels past fancy apartment blocks, bamboo stands, and jungle flowers. Passengers crane their necks for dizzying glimpses of the harbour.

The Peak Tram, originally steam-powered, was built to speed commuters to the mountainside residential areas. This was long before the dawning of the automobile age. Sedan chairs and rickshaws, the only alternatives, were slow as well as expensive. Since the tram's inauguration in 1888 it has stopped only for typhoons and World War II.

A ride on one of Hong Kong's double-decker trams is an ideal way to see the sights.

The 90-passenger cars make the journey in around eight minutes. However, on fine Saturdays and Sundays you may have to brave a crowd queueing up at the lower terminal. During the spring and autumn festivals, when the people traditionally seek out the hilltops, the throngs are so large you would be better advised to try another time; buses and taxis are also packed on such days.

At the funicular's upper terminus there is a restaurant and shopping complex resembling an airport control tower. From here you can look down on the planes taking off and landing at Hong Kong International. From the complex, you can walk around the peak in 45 minutes. On Lugard Road and

Harlech Road there are benches for a rest and an impressive view of the Hong Kong coastline.

If you're up to a climb, take the Mount Austin road to the Victoria Peak Gardens. These gardens used to belong to the governor's mountain lodge, but the building was demolished by the Japanese during the occupation of Hong Kong.

From the lower terminal of the Peak Tram it's only a short walk to the former governor's residence, now a museum. During World War II, the Japanese rebuilt this colonial building according to their own taste. From the outside it still looks eclectic, but the interior has been restored to its original colonial appearance.

Day and night — moorings off Causeway Bay teem with an assortment of boats (left). Victoria Peak offers spectacular views of the city, especially at twilight (above).

Across from the mansion, the **Zoological and Botanical Gardens** provide a welcome oasis amidst the big-city pressures. In the very early morning the park is taken over by people doing tai-chi exercises. Both young and old, go through ballet-style movements in slow motion to discipline the mind and body. The park has a modest zoo and a collection of weird and wonderful chattering jungle birds.

MORE CITY SIGHTS

Man Mo Temple is the island's oldest house of worship, though the date of its founding is subject to dispute. Visitors entering the temple are confronted by the dense pall of smoke from all the burning joss sticks and the incense coils hanging from the ceiling. The gold-plated sedan chairs on the left-hand side of the temple are used for transporting statues of the temple's gods around the neighbourhood at religious ceremonies. The statues, visible in the main shrine, represent Man and Mo, notable for their intellectual and military prowess.

The temple faces **Hollywood Road**, a street otherwise known for its shopping. Here, the windows and open doors of the shops reveal the alluring range of Asian antiques on offer — furniture, carpets, carvings, porcelain and bronze, ivory and jade. For more shopping try Western Market, near the harbour just off Connaught Road West. In this tastefully renovated Edwardian building you'll find a selection of fashionable shops and restaurants.

The aptly named Ladder Street, which intersects Hollywood Road, is a pleasure to walk along — but only if you are heading downhill. As the incline is too steep for vehicles, the roadway consists of stone steps.

Take a Tram

The ancient trolley-car system is the most leisurely and revealing way to see Hong Kong. With more than 32 km (20 miles) of track, the jerky double-deckers cover almost the entire north coast of the island. Try to get a seat on the upper deck for the best views of Hong Kong: jammed flats, rice stalls, tea shops, temples, pushcart vendors, coffin makers, umbrella factories, tape-recording counterfeiters, Chinese checker competitions, and much more.

The western terminus is in Kennedy Town, an overcrowded city in itself, named after a 19th-century Hong Kong governor, Sir Arthur Kennedy. The eastern extremity, Shau Kei Wan, once a pirates' hangout, still has a colony of "boat people" who live on junks and sampans parked in the bay.

Less than a km (half a mile) away is another popular stair-street intersecting Hollywood Road. This is Pottinger Street, lined with busy shops and stalls selling an amazing selection of buttons, bows, belts, ribbons, and braids — in fact, everything you need for dressmaking.

A devotee lights an offering in one of Hong Kong's many back-street temples.

When the lights go on in **Wanchai**, a five-minute tram ride from the financial district, you don't have to read Chinese to know what the district is selling. The neon headlines shriek "Bar," "Nightclub," and "Topless" in Chinese, English, and Japanese. Servicemen relaxing from the rigours of the Vietnam war poured millions of dollars into the Wanchai boom of the 1960s. Now office towers are replacing many of the sinful old premises.

The Wanchai waterfront is dominated by the largest **convention and exhibition centre** in Asia, which includes hotels, theatres, exhibition halls, and a recent extension that affords stunning views of the Wanchai waterfront. Another modern highlight is the **Academy for the Performing Arts**. For a total contrast, a visit to the Museum of Chinese Historical Relics is recommended (see page 39).

Causeway Bay, about 2 km (a mile) east of Wanchai, has become a prosperous tourist district with the construction of department stores and a number of good restaurants. Heavy traffic on the waterfront highway represents the border between the two aspects of the neighbourhood. On the nautical side is the Causeway Bay **typhoon shelter**, and here the rich-man–poor-man contrasts of

It takes a steady hand — an artist makes a carving in the Hollywood Road area.

Hong Kong are glaringly apparent: expensive yachts are anchored almost gunwale to gunwale with the overcrowded houseboats of the fishermen.

Opposite the World Trade Centre is the **Noonday Gun**, which under British rule was sounded on the stroke of midday. The tradition dated back more than a century. According to the legend, Jardine, Matheson & Co, a pioneer Hong Kong *hong* (trading company), fired a private salute for a visiting tycoon. This act incensed the colonial authorities, which reserved the sole right to issue a 21-gun welcome. As a result, the merchants then contritely agreed to limit their salvoes to one a day — and from then on signalled the noon hour every day for all to hear. Silent now, the Noonday Gun gave its final salute in honor of the British government at noon on July 30, 1997.

On the landward side of Causeway Bay, a hectic commercial life goes on far into the evening. In addition to several important Hong Kong, Japanese, and Chinese department stores, the area has hundreds of small shops selling clothing, food, and household goods. When restaurant, cinema, and shopping crowds all converge (and especially in the late evening when police are less likely to interfere with the proceedings), the pedestrian traffic slows down to a cheerful crawl amidst the food carts, fortune tellers, and hawkers displaying towels, toys, and trinkets. The recently renovated Hong Kong Stadium in the area hosts sports events and free, very popular Western-style concerts.

Farther inland, a branch line belonging to the tram system loops around one more district of metropolitan Hong Kong: **Happy Valley**. The name stirs mixed emotions. At one time it was a very miserable valley, a swampland conducive only to breeding malarial mosquitoes. Then the terrain was assigned to the development of the colony's first racetrack. Hong Kong gamblers are so keen to play the horses that Happy Valley is still thriving, even after the opening of a bigger and better track on the mainland at Sha Tin.

Up Tai Hang Road behind Causeway Bay is situated **Aw Boon Haw Gardens**, founded in 1935 by the late Aw Boon Haw, who became a millionaire by producing the medicinal Tiger Balm. (It does not, in fact, contain any ingredients

There are always plenty of taxis available in Hong Kong.

Ocean Park features exotic birds, as well as an "Oceanarium" said to be the largest in the world.

from tigers, but does promise to cure a wide range of problems such as colds, headaches, rheumatism, gout, toothache, and scorpion bites.) With its garish pagodas, artificial caves, and brightly painted statues of well-known Taoist and Buddhist legends, the garden is an obvious setting for attractive souvenir photos.

ROUND THE COAST

Aberdeen, the island's oldest settlement, is also home to its largest "floating population" — the thousands of people who spend their entire lives on the junks and sampans in the **harbour**. It makes for a blaze of local colour: barefoot children frolicking on the poop deck, women hanging up the laundry or playing mah-jong, elderly folk watching the sunset, dogs and cats underfoot, songbirds in bamboo cages overhead … and all afloat.

There are water taxis galore, including small sampans with women drivers who propel the craft by hand, like gondoliers. You will doubtless be offered a sampan tour of the choked port, from where you can just glimpse the few remaining boatyards of Ap Lei Chau island. You can cross the flyover (overpass) to visit the island, but there is little to see since the decline of the boat-building industry.

Aberdeen's floating restaurants have attracted tourists for many years. The raw materials for the restaurants are impressive; if you can't make it to the pre-dawn auction held at the vast local wholesale **fish market**, have a look at the retail street market later in the day.

Near the bus terminal is a temple built by local fishermen in 1851. It is dedicated to Tin Hau, the Queen of Heaven and Patroness of Seafarers. Originally the temple was on the shore but reclamation projects have now left it high and dry. On the 23rd day of the Third Moon, the birthday of the patroness Taoist goddess is celebrated here and in all Hong Kong fishing communities.

The peninsula opposite the east coast of Ap Lei Chau island has been developed, and contains **Ocean Park**, Middle Kingdom and Water World. Ocean Park has become one of Hong Kong's greatest attractions. The Oceanarium is said to be the largest in the world, and features displays by dolphins, killer whales, seals, and pelicans. An enormous roller-coaster rising way above the sea, space wheels, high-diving shows, and the longest outdoor escalator in the world guarantee a day of excitement. Linking the lowland and highland sections of the park, a cable-car system offers spectacular views across to the islands of the South China Sea.

Situated next to Ocean Park is the somewhat more sedate **Middle Kingdom**. Here is a "living" history of China which is presented through a number of full-size replicas of shrines, temples, pagodas, palaces, and street scenes. Also on offer are fascinating demonstrations of traditional Chinese crafts, including silk weaving, pottery, and paper making.

A sandy beach leads you to **Water World**, a large wave-pool connected to several others. There are also fast-food shops and a Chinese restaurant to ensure that you do not go hungry. Water World is open throughout the summer months.

Continuing round the coast in an anti-clockwise direction: Deep Water Bay offers a good beach and harbours an enviable flotilla of resident sailboats and yachts. The next inlet, **Repulse Bay** is more famous. The roomy, sandy crescent, backed by green hills, is so attractive and so easy to reach that it is packed with sunbathers all summer long.

Stanley was once one of the main fishing villages on Hong Kong Island. Today it has developed into a thriving market town and a popular residential area. The market, selling overrun designer jeans and clothes in Western sizes, as well as brassware, porcelain, and Chinese handicrafts, is a mecca for bargain hunters. The seafront at Repulse Bay and Stanley is lined with very nice cafés and restaurants.

KOWLOON

Though much smaller than Hong Kong island, Kowloon has almost twice the population. In many streets the density reaches the equivalent of 150,000 inhabitants per square km (quarter square mile), an appalling crush of humanity over-flowing onto the tenement roofs.

Most of Kowloon's attractions for visitors are centred near the tip of the peninsula in the district known as **Tsimshatsui**. Near the Star Ferry terminal the dust has been flying in a

Squid , dried on racks, and almost every type of local fish are on sale in Aberdeen's markets.

frenzy of redevelopment of the waterfront district. This is where you'll find the **Hong Kong Space Museum**, with its futuristic architecture.

Still more imposing, the **Hong Kong Cultural Centre** has a controversial windowless façade and bowed roofline. Hong Kong's largest venue for the performing arts, it contains a concert hall with acclaimed acoustics, two theatres, an exhibition gallery, shops, restaurants, and bars.

Further raising the cultural level is the Museum of Art. West of Star Ferry pier is Harbour City, Asia's biggest shopping centre, and next to it is China Hong Kong City, a complex that contains shopping arcades and a ferry terminal to mainland China and Macau.

In an unusual move towards conservation, a historic (early 20th-century) clock tower of the original Kowloon-Canton

Kowloon's clock tower is all that remains of the old Kowloon-Canton railway terminal.

Railway terminal has escaped demolition. The terminal itself was torn down after being replaced by a new one about a mile away in Hung Hom. Part of the relocated station complex is the modern Hong Kong Coliseum, claimed to be the largest indoor air-conditioned auditorium in Asia.

The most exciting view of the Kowloon peninsula must be the one witnessed from an aeroplane coming in to land at Kai Tak, alias Hong Kong International Airport. The plane's final approach is so low over the rooftops that passengers can see laundry hanging out like flags on the bamboo poles jutting from every room. The runway has been built on land reclaimed from the sea.

In another reclamation project, more than 60 hectares (150 acres) of new land were created. These became Tsimshatsui East, a vital commercial district. Luxurious hotels are found in TST East, as are multi-storey shopping plazas, nightspots, and office buildings. The waterfront promenade offers a fine view of Hong Kong island.

Nathan Road, Kowloon's main street, was created when Sir Matthew Nathan was governor of Hong Kong (1904–1907). At the time it was built, many thought it ab-

HONG KONG MUSEUM HIGHLIGHTS

For opening times see page 119.

Flagstaff House Museum of Tea Ware, Victoria Barracks, Cotton Tree Drive, Hong Kong. An unusual collection of Chinese tea sets dating from the fifth century b.c. to the present.

Fung Ping Shan Museum of Hong Kong University, 94 Bonham Road, Hong Kong. From ancient Chinese pottery to nearly a thousand early Christian crosses, plus paintings, sculpture, and bronzes.

Hong Kong Museum of Art, City Hall, 10th and 11th floors. Rotating exhibitions provide a crash course in Chinese ceramics, bronzes, jade, and paintings — including pictures documenting Sino-British relations.

Hong Kong Museum of History, Kowloon Park. A brief survey of local culture and customs from prehistory to modern times, illustrating everything from fishing techniques and farming to architecture and handicrafts.

Hong Kong Space Museum, Salisbury Road, Kowloon, contains an exhibition hall, with push-button displays, videos, and picture boards tracing the history of astronomy. The Space Theatre has daily film showings on a huge Omnimax screen.

Lei Cheng Uk Museum, Tonkin Street, Kowloon. An ancient burial vault discovered inside a hillock during construction work: the 2,000-year-old Han tomb is now protected behind glass. In the small museum you can view funerary objects found on the site.

Museum of Chinese Historical Relics, 1st floor, Causeway Centre, 28 Harbour Road, Wanchai. Displays of cultural treasures from China, with temporary exhibitions from specific provinces scheduled.

Jade, in every shape and size is available at stall after stall at Kowloon's famous jade market.

surd to have a tree-lined boulevard running through what was practically a wilderness. Now the former "Nathan's Folly" is called the "Golden Mile." The glittering hotels, restaurants, nightclubs, and shops along its length constantly attract crowds.

Yau Ma Tei, at the northern end of Nathan Road, is one of the older parts of Kowloon, and is renowned for its temples and typhoon shelters. It is also the site of Kowloon's famous **jade market** — a shopping phenomenon held every day from 10:00 A.M. to 3:30 P.M. in a section of Kansu Street. Vendors of jade, a stone which has had special meaning for the Chinese for centuries, spread their trinkets and treasures over the pavement. Nearby, off Jordan Road, is **Temple Street Night Market**, the lively night-time venue for fortune tellers and Chinese opera singers, jostling for space with street vendors of all kinds — especially purveyors of CDs and pornographic videos from the West.

In North Kowloon (in Lai Chi Kok Road) is a re-creation of a **Sung Dynasty Village**. This is a full-sized model village with houses, shops, temples, and gardens of the Sung dynasty (A.D. 960–1279). "Villagers" in traditional costume provide entertainments, including displays of martial arts and music and dance. Chinese artists and artisans show how they work; historical personages fill a wax museum; and, of course, Chinese food is featured as well.

NEW TERRITORIES

Hong Kong's New Territories begin at Boundary Street. Surprises spring up on all sides: new industrial complexes alongside sleepy farming villages, skyscraper towns blooming in the middle of nowhere, women in coolie hats tending to their water buffalo, and flashes of azalea everywhere. Ask the tourist authority for information on tours from Kowloon.

The highway makes a circuit of the New Territories, beginning with the new town of Tsuen Wan, situated in an area of heavy industry just west of Kowloon. North of the town, a

---

Wild and Beautiful

Remote areas of the New Territories are happy sighting grounds for birdwatchers. Hundreds of species have been recorded, from everyday egrets and funny-faced cockatoos to mynahs and pelicans.

As civilization encroaches, wild animals have been vanishing: leopards have not been seen here in 20 years. But you can still come across barking deer, monkeys, porcupines, and scaly anteaters. In the wilderness you may also stumble upon a banded krait, a cobra, or some other fearsome snake. Though sightings are common, bitings are rare.

commanding view over all the New Territories to the north can be seen from Tai Mo Shan, Hong Kong's highest peak at 957 metres (3,140 feet). The highway continues parallel to the coast. One-third of all Hong Kong's beaches are to be found in a single 14-km (9-mile) stretch of this region's shoreline. Place names are often based on the distance to the nearest mile-post, as measured from the tip of the Kowloon peninsula. Thus you will find "19½-mile beach" at Castle Peak Bay.

At the 21 milestone, near the large new town of Tuen Mun, is a Taoist retreat known as **Ching Chung Koon**. This "Temple of Green Pines" is a spacious complex containing temples and pavilions, statues and gardens. It is known for its collection of bonsai (miniature plants) and also houses a number of Chinese art treasures, including a jade seal more than 1,000 years old. Among the ponds is one inhabited by turtles. Visitors toss in coins in the hope of bouncing one off a turtle's head — a sure way of achieving good fortune.

The main road continues clockwise round the New Territories and on to the big market town of Yuen Long (the centre for a boisterous trade in live ducks). A side road leads to the coastal village of Lau Fau Shan on Deep Bay. The townsfolk work the local oyster beds which supply Hong Kong with fresh shellfish and export markets with dried oysters and oyster sauce. On offer in the village restaurants you will find all manner of dishes based on the local delicacy — but don't eat the oysters raw.

Much of the area beyond Yuen Long is given over to fish ponds and duck ponds, conjuring up a moody scene that seems to belong to a China of long ago. Another image right out of Chinese history is the walled village of **Kat Hing Wai**, situated about 3 km (2 miles) east of Yuen Long, within the village of Kam Tin. It is built in a square, and the only way in is through the gate in the brick defensive wall, where

*Smiling Hakka women of Kat Hing Wai cheerfully
pose for a photograph.*

tourists are invited to make a contribution "for the welfare of the village." Kat Hing Wai was built four or five centuries ago by the Hakka people, who migrated from North China. You see Hakkas throughout the New Territories; the women can be identified by their flat straw hats which have black "curtains" hanging round the rim. Women in black clothing sit around the entrance to the Kat Hing Wai compound playing cards, occasionally dropping out to tend one of the souvenir stalls. Incidentally, in this old village everyone belongs to the same clan, so they all have the same surname, Tang.

The lookout point at Lok Ma Chau was long known as Hong Kong's "window on China" — a view over the Shenzhen River, duck ponds, and paddy fields into the daily life of villagers in Guangdong Province.

In the years of China's isolation from the West, tourists would come to the lookout point here and rent binoculars in order to get a glimpse of the great mystery beyond. Now that China has embraced foreign tourism, as well as Hong Kong itself, much of the drama has dissipated.

On the journey back to Kowloon, the highway and the railway stay close together from Fanling, the site of the best golf courses in the country. The railway line then curves gracefully around **Tolo Harbour**, an idyllic body of water well protected from the open sea. You can take a ferryboat through the harbour, past the ingenious **Plover Cove** reservoir, a water catchment area appropriated from the sea by damming and draining a broad inlet. The boats go on to the friendly fishermen's island of Tap Mun, in Mirs Bay, with stops in various remote hamlets of the **Sai Kung Peninsula**. The Sai Kung area is the location of two official country parks, while on the south side of the peninsula are some of the territory's best beaches.

From the next railway station, University, the modern campus of the Chinese University of Hong Kong is visible. Unlike the older, British-style University of Hong Kong (at Pokfulam on Hong Kong island), the Chinese University

Thirsty Territory

Those huge black pipes you see here and there in the New Territories are pumping Chinese water to the Hong Kong waterworks. Fresh water from Guangdong Province, purified in Hong Kong, accounts for about one-quarter of the territory's entire supply.

All the ingenious, multi-billion-dollar reservoirs, plus a costly desalination plant, can't guarantee that the supply will always equal the demand. In times of drought, Hong Kong has to limit the times when consumers may turn on the tap.

conducts its teaching in both Chinese and English.

Sha Tin is the site of the Monastery of 10,000 Buddhas, which looks down on a burgeoning town. There are hundreds of stone steps in the hillside to walk up before you reach **Man Fat Temple**, with its regiments of small gilt statues of Buddha lining the walls. Some indefatigable climbers will want to go up to the top of the nine-storey pink pagoda for a panoramic view. There is a total of 12,800 Buddha statues here, plus the remains of the monastery's founder, embalmed in gold leaf.

Down to earth, the **Sha Tin Racecourse**, which came in at a mere HK$500 million, can cater for over

Visitors climb the nine-storey pagoda at Man Fat Temple to enjoy the spectacular view.

80,000 spectators and is equipped with every imaginable touch of luxury, including a giant video screen facing the stands. For the horses there are air-conditioned stables and even a swimming pool. Opposite the Sha Tin railway station, **New Town Plaza** features shops, cinemas, and even a computer-controlled musical fountain.

Two natural rock formations are always pointed out on excursions. Sha Tin Rock, better known as **Amah Rock**, is actually a pile of several rocks which resemble a woman with a baby in a sling on her back. Legend has it that a local woman climbed the hill every day to watch for her husband returning from across the sea; one day the wife and her child were turned to stone, as a permanent symbol of her enduring faith.

Closer to town is **Lion Rock**, shaped like a lion lying in wait. It's an unusual rock formation in that it really looks the part; the tourists know its name even before the guide can translate it.

ISLANDS

Excursion companies sell a variety of orientation cruises of Hong Kong harbour that include a look at some if its 235 outlying islands. These pleasant, but expensive, outings can lay the foundation for your own explorations aboard the cheap but usually comfortable ferries used by the islanders themselves. From the ferry terminals on the overpopulated north coast of Hong Kong island you can escape to islands without cars or cares, where the local people smile "hello" and, if you're lucky, point you towards a secret beach.

☞ Lantau Island

Lantau is the biggest island in the colony, and covers nearly twice the area of Hong Kong island, though its population is a mere 25,000. All those wide open spaces, barely 9 km (6 miles) east of Hong Kong, explain the rush of city folk there on weekends and holidays.

At 934 metres (3,064 feet), Lantau Peak is high enough to attract the occasional raincloud — and refreshingly cool breezes blow on most hot summer days. The biggest community on the island, **Tai O**, makes its living by fishing, duck-breeding, and food processing. Many of the inhabitants live, in one way or another, on the water — aboard house-boats or in houses on stilts in the main creek.

Ferryboats from Hong Kong go to three Lantau ports; the closest is at Silvermine Bay on the east coast. The village of Silvermine Bay (Mui Wo), with a sagging old drawbridge across the inlet and incongruous eight-storey buildings, is not quite up to picture-postcard standards. However, it is only a short bus ride to the more appealing **Cheung Sha Beach**, some 3 km (2 miles) long, and popular for its white sand and excellent facilities.

A bus service also links Silvermine Bay with Lantau's famous Buddhist monastery. The road, overlooked by one of the world's largest outdoor bronze Buddhas, climbs steep, scenic hillsides to reach the **Po Lin Monastery**. Here, grey-

The beach at Lamma Island is the perfect place to get away from it all.

Lamma's restaurants offer a wide selection of good, home-style Chinese food.

robed monks with shaven heads float past picnickers (who are informed by signs in Chinese and English not to bring with them any meat, as these are vegetarian premises). The large, modern Buddhist hall is only one of several shrines at Po Lin. The hillsides that surround the monastery are the site of Hong Kong's only tea plantation. Visitors are welcome to visit the 24-hectare (60-acre) establishment, and may sample the end product, Lantau tea.

Nearby, a **Trappist monastery**, situated on a hillside overlooking the east coast of Lantau, is also open to visitors. To get there, take the commuter ferry that sails from Hong Kong to Peng Chau (a small island just off Lantau), and then take the monastery's shuttle ferry. Finally, a 15-minute uphill walk from the jetty brings you to the monastery. The Trappists, who fled Peking during the Chinese civil war, have been living on Lantau since their monastery was completed in 1956.

Many hikers enjoy the two-hour cross-country trek from the monastery down to Silvermine Bay, but the authorities have warned walkers to be on the lookout for snakes, which can be plentiful in the Lantau hinterland, especially in summer. There are likely to be big changes throughout the area, though, with the recent completion of Hong Kong's new Chek Lapkok Airport on a small island opposite Tung Chung village.

Cheung Chau

Some 10 km (6 miles) west of Hong Kong lies this small island of about 30,000 people, mostly fishermen, which has had a chequered past in the smuggling and piracy business. That era has gone now, but other elements of the island's simple old life are nicely preserved. The people still carve jade and build seaworthy junks, all by hand. Fish (heads discreetly wrapped in paper) are still hung out to dry in the sun. No one minds; not even the business-suited expatriates who have settled on this traffic-free island and take the ferry to their offices in noisy, high-rent Hong Kong.

Cheung Chau becomes the centre of Hong Kong life once a year, usually in May, during the Bun Festival, a folklore extravaganza (see page 79). During the rest of the year, life goes on at its accustomed pace: with rickety machines chugging in two-man factories, children in spotless school uniforms being ferried back home to houseboats, and the old fishermen stirring shrimp paste.

By way of formal tourist attractions, **Pak Tai Temple** has some fine carvings and a great iron sword said to be 600 years old. The temple, built in 1783, is dedicated to a Taoist sea divinity, who is believed to have rescued the villagers from a plague. Pak Tai Temple is only a short walk from the ferry landing. The island has several other temples and shrines as well as some good beaches and, of course, there is plenty of fresh seafood.

Lamma Island

Situated only 3 km (2 miles) off the southwest coast of Hong Kong island is the getaway island of Lamma — perfect for swimming, hiking, picnicking, birdwatching, or just sitting back to watch the bananas grow.

Lamma island is a suitably peaceful setting for this shrine overlooking the sea.

Life on Lamma, if not totally primitive, gets close to the essentials. There are no cars, not even motorcycles, and the few bicycles to be seen have nowhere much to go.

The area is only less than one-fifth the size of Hong Kong island, and none of the villages has hardly more than a few hundred inhabitants.

Archaeological findings indicate that Lamma has probably been inhabited for some 4,000 years, and the island is known somewhat glamorously as "Hong Kong's Stone Age Island."

Ferries from Central go to **Yung Shue Wan**, the principal settlement of Lamma's northwest, or to **Sok Kwu Wan**, on the east coast. Both villages offer good waterfront restaurants with homestyle Chinese food, principally seafood fresh from the tank. The ports are within hiking distance of several beautiful beaches. You can build up an appetite for dinner, by making your way from the beach to the restaurant. Yung Shue Wan is still somewhat of a British residential enclave, with many nice pubs.

You can return to the modern world on board the creaky old ferry that crosses to Aberdeen. The voyage is brief but stimulating, as transistorized picnickers on a visit from the big city mingle with islanders carrying anything from large oil drums and free-roaming chickens to caged snakes.

EXCURSIONS

Macau

Macau, the final bastion of Portugal's great 16th-century empire, is much more than just a quirk of history. Here, where East and West first met, life combines the spirit of Asia with the lazy, sunny atmosphere of the Mediterranean.

In this unique situation, the incongruous becomes routine: the latest jetfoil skimming past traditional junks; a Chinese temple alongside a Portuguese fortress; computerized betting on an ancient ball game; and trucks and buses with twin licence plates — black-and-white ones from Macau, yellow and black from China.

For a number of years the Portuguese foothold on Macau has been as precarious as an egret's status on the back of a rhi-

These Macau fishing boats have cast their nets away from the heavy traffic that typifies the waters around Hong Kong.

The impressive bridge to Macau — the island reverts to Chinese rule in 1999.

noceros. China is 600,000 times bigger than Macau. Recently, Macau's 16 square km (6 square miles), together with its two offshore islands, have been officially termed a Chinese territory under Portuguese administration. But that is due to end in 1999, when the enclave reverts to direct Chinese rule.

Macau's population is an estimated 450,000; an appallingly high figure for such a small area. Yet the visitor feels little of the sardine-tin complex of Hong Kong, 64 km (40 miles) away, where there sometimes seems no room to breathe. The traffic jams in Macau, mercifully, are still 10 years behind the rest of the world. A trace of tropical lethargy adds to the charm in this city of sidewalk cafés, palm trees, pedicabs, peeling pink-and-green buildings, and blind fortune-tellers under the arcades. But the torpor definitely ends once inside the doors of Macau's casinos, scene of some of the liveliest gambling west of Las Vegas.

The story of the Western discovery of Macau began in 1513 when Portuguese explorer, Jorge Alvares, reached the

The Ruins of St. Paul's — only the façade is left of this once-grand Jesuit Church on Macau.

hillside. Opposite the temple is the Maritime Museum, which explains in detail the maritime history of the area.

In contrast, the very secular Macau Palace, a floating casino, is moored on the western waterfront. The fancifully decorated multi-storey barge goes nowhere, and is fitted out with gambling tables, slot machines (which are known locally as "hungry tigers"), and, for hungry humans, a restaurant.

For an authentic feel of old Portugal, slip into the cool entrance hall of the **Leal Senado** ("Loyal Senate" building), situated on the main street. On the walls are flowered blue tiles (*azulejos*) and noble coats of arms. The inscription over the archway reads, "*Cidade do nome de Deus, não ha outra mais leal*" (City of the Name of God, None is More Loyal) — a bit of praise attributed to Portugal's King John IV in the 17th century. For all its historic grandeur, the loyal Senate now is the equivalent of a city council, its statesmanship dedicated to

The streets of Macau are rich with history and architectural diversity.

water supplies, sewage lines, and the establishment of playgrounds.

Macau's most memorable monument, the **Ruins of St. Paul's**, is a Baroque façade, the only remains of a beautiful 17th-century Jesuit church. The rest of the building and an adjoining college were destroyed in a typhoon-fanned fire in 1835. The rich sculptural effects on the façade mix Eastern and Western symbols: familiar saints, Chinese dragons, and a Portuguese caravel.

Luís Vaz de Camões (1524–1580), the Portuguese national poet whose work immortalized that country's golden age of discoveries, may have stayed in Macau. Local legend claims that he wrote part of his great saga, *Os Lusíadas*, in what is now called the Camões Grotto, situated in the spacious tropical **Camões Garden**.

Behind the elaborate exterior of this Macau casino, the tables are busy 24 hours a day.

village of Coloane, the waterfront drive parallels the shore of a Chinese island. A busy Chinese quarry is just across the thin strip of sea, which is patrolled by Chinese boats.

The Catholic Church of St. Francis Xavier has on display the elbow of the saint (a 16th-century missionary, and patron saint of all Catholic missionaries), along with the bones of numerous Japanese and Vietnamese martyrs.

Lucky Macau

The non-stop excitement of the casinos involves familiar international games — including baccarat, blackjack, boule, craps, roulette, and more exotic Chinese pastimes. Watch the fantan dealer for a few minutes and you'll almost be an expert. It's simply a matter of how many odd buttons are left after he has divided a pile of them into groups of four.

Dai-Siu (Big and Small) is a dice game in which the croupier throws three dice inside a glass container. Players bet on the numbers that will come up, and on whether the result will be

There is always a fascinating range of unfamiliar foods on display in the local shops.

"big" or "small." *Keno* is a variation of bingo in which the player chooses numbers to bet on before the draw is made.

The casinos have no admission charge and formal dress is optional. Employees of the Macau government are barred from the casinos except during three days at the lunar New Year. A proliferation of pawn shops indicates that no one can win every time.

The casinos keep busy 24 hours a day, but if you want a change of scene there are always more gambling opportunities available. You can try your luck at pari mutuel betting on *jai-alai* (the high-speed Basque game), greyhound racing at the Canidrome (one of the largest in the world), and harness racing on Taipa island.

Shopping in Macau

Browsing is a real pleasure in Macau's main streets and byways, where shops aimed at the tourist market are interspersed with the more workaday ironmongers, herbalists, and noodle stalls. Knowledgeable visitors look for antiques — either Chinese heirlooms or leftovers from the gracious Portuguese colonial days. Jewellery and gold are both good buys. Also worth investigating are contemporary handicrafts, both Portuguese and Chinese from across the border.

Food and Drink

Gourmets award Macau high marks for dependable Chinese cooking with an exotic bonus: Portuguese food and wines. Whether you choose to dine in one of the Chinese, Portuguese, or international-style restaurants, you will be treated to a hearty meal at a good price.

The ingredients, especially the fresh fish and seafood, are first-rate. Your chopsticks will never have dissected a more delicate, delicious fish than the Macau sole (*linguado*). Imported dried cod (*bacalhao*) is the Portuguese national dish; several varieties are available, usually baked.

Macau has an ample, happily priced supply of Portuguese wines. Try a *vinho verde* — a slightly sparkling young wine from northern Portugal — or a hearty red *Dão* or *Colares*. After dinner, a glass of Madeira or Port is recommended to round off the meal. The more abstemious can stick to Portuguese mineral water.

See page 114 for practical information on Macau.

Former Border Zones

For Hong Kong visitors with little time to spare for planning or for sightseeing, various tour agencies run day-trips to the area just across the border for a hint of the "real" China. Although the farm country there is typically Chinese, the city of Shenzhen is not; it is part of a special economic zone devised to attract foreign investment, and its standard of living is far higher than average.

Day-trips across the frontier from Macau usually include a visit to the village of Cuiheng, the birthplace of Dr. Sun Yat-sen, father of modern China.

☛ Guangzhou (Canton)

Foreigners have been arriving in Guangzhou for a couple of thousand years, for it was the country's first major seaport. This has made for some dramatic historical incidents: the Opium Wars, for instance, broke out because of a crackdown in Canton. The city still maintains its important gateway role. Ever since 1957 the Canton Trade Fair (officially the Chinese Export Commodities Fair) has attracted throngs of international business people every spring and autumn. Even when tourism dwindled almost to zero because of political upheavals, Guangzhou kept open the nation's ties with foreign countries as well as with overseas Chinese.

Guangzhou (with a population around five million) straddles the Pearl River — China's fifth longest — which links the city to the South China Sea. This waterway accounts for much of the local charm and excitement, as the daily drama of the ferryboats, junks, sampans, freighters — and even the small tankers and big gunboats — unfolds right in the centre of town. The river also irrigates the carefully tended surrounding farmlands, creating a beautifully lush, subtropical scene.

What to See

Package tours to Guangzhou have a fairly standard itinerary. However, there is no objection to your leaving a specific excursion and roaming on your own within the city limits. A typical four-day schedule contains sightseeing by coach and boat, excursions to a farming community or an industrial town, a theatre outing, and a full-scale Chinese banquet. Alternatively, you can travel independently by bus from Hong Kong.

Zhenhai Tower, one of Guangzhou's oldest buildings, now houses the municipal museum.

Yuexiu Park, situated near the Trade Fair in the northern part of the city, covers a hilly 92 hectares (229 acres). In addition to pretty gardens, lakes, and sports facilities, Guangzhou's largest park also contains one of the city's oldest buildings, **Zhenhai Tower**. To be exact, "tower" is a misleading name for this five-storey building with verandahs, but because of its hilltop position it was once used as an ancient watchtower. Built in 1380, it now houses the municipal museum, with its emphasis on Guangzhou's history and art.

In Yuexiu Park is an **obelisk** about 30 metres (100 feet) tall honouring Dr. Sun Yat-sen (1866–1925), who began his political career in Canton. South of the park is an even more impres-

For a taste of China, take a trip over the border to its most visited city, Guangzhou (Canton).

sive **monument** to him built in 1931 with contributions from overseas Chinese. This enormous, modern version of a traditional Chinese building, with sweeping blue tile roofs, contains an auditorium big enough to seat almost 5,000 people.

Guangzhou's most important Buddhist monument, the **Temple of the Six Banyan Trees**, was founded over 1,400 years ago. Although today the trees which inspired an 11th-century poet and calligrapher to rename the Precious Solemnity Temple are no more, the often-restored complex has remained a focus of local Buddhist activities. Overlooking it is the 17-storey **Flower Pagoda**, a slender relic of the Sung dynasty (A.D. 960–1279).

In the early Middle Ages, Canton had a significant Muslim population, as a result of its trade with the Middle East. This explains the presence in Guangzhou of the **Huaisheng Mosque**, reputed to be China's oldest and traditionally dated

A.D. 627. It has been rebuilt in modern times and, after a hiatus during the Cultural Revolution, is now once more serving the small local community of Muslims. The modern **minaret** is known as the Plain (or Naked) Pagoda, in contrast to the Flower Pagoda of the Buddhist temple.

Another of the city's religious edifices that experienced hard times in the 1960s and 1970s is the Roman Catholic **cathedral**. Red Guards converted the century-old Gothic building into a warehouse, but it was returned to its original use and reconsecrated in 1979.

The atmosphere of 19th-century Canton is best evoked on **Shamian Island**, in the Pearl River, which is linked to central Guangzhou by two bridges. This small formerly residential island, beautifully shaded by banyan trees, was the home of the closed community of the foreign colony in the era of the "concessions." Now, its stately European-style buildings have been taken over for use as government offices, foreign legations, or public housing. The churches have been assigned the most prosaic uses. One is a warehouse with pews, and its stained-glass windows have been acquired by the neighbouring houses. A haunting, nostalgic place, the island now has a modern luxury hotel.

A popular optional excursion is an hour's detour to **Guangzhou Zoo**, founded in 1958. It houses more than 200 animal species, most famous of which is the giant panda, and has an imaginative monkey mountain behind a moat.

Revolutionary Monuments

Guided tours of Guangzhou usually include one or more of the following sites which have been linked with revolutionary activity in the city's history.

A former Confucian temple is the home of the **National Peasant Movement Institute**, where the Chinese Communist Party trained its corps of leaders in the 1920s. Mao Ze-dong himself directed the institute in 1926, and gave lectures on geography, rural education, and "The Problem of the Chinese Peasantry." Zhou Enlai also taught here.

Martyrs Memorial Park — more formally known as the Memorial Park to the Martyrs of the Guangzhou Uprising — was dedicated on the 30th anniversary of the doomed insurrection of 11 December, 1927. The armed uprising against the Kuomintang, led by the Communist Party, was over within three days, crushed at a cost of more than 5,000 lives. Most of the park consists of lawns and flower gardens, palm trees, and pavilions, so it's an especially relaxing place to watch the locals strolling or playing Chinese checkers.

Another memorial park surrounds the **Mausoleum of the 72 Martyrs**, dedicated to victims of one of the insurrections that failed in 1911, only a few months before Dr. Sun Yat-sen's successful revolution. The design of the monumental ensemble has something to suit all tastes: Chinese lions, an Egyptian obelisk, even a model of the Statue of Liberty.

Excursion to Foshan

A very popular day-trip from Guangzhou goes to **Foshan**, a city of nearly 300,000 people, renowned over the centuries for its handicrafts. Here, you can see silk weaving, a ceramics plant, and the Foshan Folk Art Studio, where you can observe workers making Chinese lanterns, carving sculptures, painting scrolls, and cutting intricate designs in paper.

Foshan's most outstanding artistic monument is the Taoist Ancestral Temple, a Sung dynasty establishment rebuilt in the 14th century. Constructed in wood, brick, stone, ceramics, and bronze, this is a work of extravagant beauty, uniting many ancient art forms.

See also page 111 for practical information on Guangzhou.

WHAT TO DO

SHOPPING

Though inflation takes its toll here as much as anywhere else, Hong Kong's reputation for bargains is well founded. However, the main difference between Hong Kong and other duty-free ports is the great variety of goods on offer here.

The favourite buys in Hong Kong fall into two main categories: the duty-free imported goods—including photographic equipment, electronic goods, and watches—on which you avoid the luxury tax payable in your home country, and the specialist goods, usually hand-made, from Hong Kong and elsewhere in China, including souvenirs and custom-made garments run up by skillful Hong Kong tailors.

One of the best buys in Hong Kong is high-tech photographic equipment.

When and Where

Stores do not open until 10:00 A.M. but shopping goes on into the evening (except in Central and Western, where closing time is 6:00 P.M.). The last ones to shut are Causeway Bay, Wanchai, and City Plaza—at 9:30 P.M. Most shops, except for some in Central, open seven days a week.

> **Hong Kong is also called the "Manhattan of the Orient" because of its shopping, its food, and its skyline.**

The only holiday on which all commerce comes to a halt is the Chinese New Year in January or February.

You'll find that prices are about the same in Hong Kong and Kowloon. Large shops on the fashionable thoroughfares

Traditional Chinese medicines are available in pharmacies such as this one in Macau.

tend to be more expensive than smaller "family" shops tucked away in the side streets.

If you want a more unusual shopping trip, don't miss the street markets with their unexpected bargains and bazaar-like atmosphere. The items on sale include clothing over-runs, particularly shirts, tracksuits, sweaters, and denim. One of the most promising concentrations of likely bargains is in Stanley, and the Temple Street Night Market in Yau Ma Tei provides brightly lit stalls to tempt the nocturnal shopper.

Department stores that sell Chinese products are found in all the major shopping areas. Their fascinating merchandise is also very attractively priced. Look out especially for their art, toys, and food.

Buyer Beware

All the large department stores post their prices, and these are fixed. However, elsewhere you should ask whether there is a discount. In many shops haggling is the order of the day, but never buy any significant item without comparing prices first, and beware of touts who offer to take you to wondrous bargains. If the price goes absurdly low you may be dealing with second-hand or falsely labelled goods. Always ask to see the manufacturer's guarantee when purchasing watches, cameras, and audio-visual and electronic equipment. For any major purchase you should always obtain a receipt recording information about the item and, if appropriate, shipping and insurance details. It's wise to contact your local customs office for information concerning import duties and regulations before leaving home.

Note that when haggling, the merchant assumes you are prepared to pay cash. If, after concluding a deal, you try to pay with a credit card, he may then boost the price in order to cover the card charges.

It is advisable to shop at outlets which are members of the Hong Kong Tourist Association (these are identified by the red junk logo on prominent display). Membership imposes an obligation to maintain standards of both quality and service, and provides dissatisfied customers with an officially recognized channel for prompt redress of complaints.

Note that alcohol and tobacco are both exceptions to Hong Kong's duty-free régime and are subject to tax.

What to Buy

Antiques: One centre for antique dealers is the Hollywood Road area, but there are others to be found in all the tourist shopping zones. Look out for fine Chinese bronzes, embroidery, lacquerware and porcelain, and wood carving, among other possibilities. The experts point out that it is not only the age of a Chinese antique that determines its value, as dynasties had their creative ups and downs. Although haggling is frowned upon, discounts can often be obtained. Meanwhile, beware of convincing modern imitations being passed off as real antiques.

Brocades and silks: Fabrics from China—inexpensive raw silk or exquisite brocades—are well worth taking home. Chinese-product department stores stock silk scarves, ties, finely embroidered blouses, and traditional padded jackets.

Cameras: Photo buffs know that Hong Kong is the place to buy some of the world's most advanced photographic equipment, and there are some real bargains around. However, be sure you compare prices and models before buying.

Carpets and rugs: A mecca for Chinese hand-knotted wool carpets and silk rugs, Hong Kong's stores are usually able to arrange shipment.

China: In Hong Kong you can have a plate, or even a whole dinner service, hand-painted to your own design. Factories

You'll find many beautiful antiques on sale in Hong Kong—but beware of fakes!

in Kowloon and the New Territories, producing traditional and modern china, are geared to entertain and instruct visiting tourists; prices are appealing. In antiques shops, look for highly valued porcelains from China. Surprisingly, good bargains may be found in the best makes of European china, including Spode and Wedgwood, because of the duty-free situation in Hong Kong.

Computers: Both imported and local computers are competitively priced and represent good value for money.

Electronic equipment: Miniaturization increases the convenience of the latest gadgets, while Hong Kong obligingly subtracts tax from the price.

Furniture: The choice ranges from traditional hand-carved Chinese rosewood furniture to well-made reproductions of modern Western styles. Rattan furniture is highly popular.

Jade: "Good for the health" is just one of the many magical qualities that are attributed to these beautiful emerald-green or turquoise stones. This explains the constant demand for jade that keeps its prices up. You may be offered counterfeit jade, which looks exactly like the genuine article. Some people say

Jewellery is one of the best purchases to make while in Hong Kong.

you can test the authenticity by touch—real jade feels smooth and cool. Alternatively, you can shine a lamp on the stone—real jade shows no reflected light. If all else fails, you could try licking it: real jade makes the tongue feel numb. Better still, go shopping with an expert, or patronize a respectable shop.

Jewellery: Thanks to the duty-free situation, prices in Hong Kong are among some of the lowest in the world. You can buy gemstones loose or set, or have them made up to your own design. Popular purchases include diamonds and freshwater pearls. If you do plan to buy jewellery, be sure to seek out a reputable dealer or first consult the *Shopping Guide to Jewellery* published by the Hong Kong Tourist Authority.

Leather goods: You can have your clothes, shoes, handbags, or luggage specially made to measure, and there is also a wide range of locally produced and imported leather accessories choose from—all at extremely attractive prices.

Mah-jong sets: Ivory sets are extremely expensive, but tiles of bone or plastic have a certain charm when they've been engraved by hand. As you'll know from the familiar sound of clickety-clack coming from every second window in Hong Kong, mah-jong is one of the most popular local vices.

Musical, audio, and video equipment: Hong Kong has a vast range of the most high-tech audio-visual, sound, and screen equipment to choose from. Video cassette recorders, portable camcorders, compact disc players, and mini-TVs are good bargains, but be sure to look round before buying, as dealers often try to get rid of last year's models first. Before purchase, visitors should also ensure compatibility with the broadcasting system in their own country. Whatever you choose to buy, you may be able to work out a discount.

Perfumes: You will find a wide selection of brand-name fragrances available in Hong Kong at favourable prices. To avoid counterfeits it is wise to head for the major shops.

Ready-to-wear clothes: Hong Kong is one of the world's top clothing producers—mainly for the export market. Factory outlets sell fashion overruns at reasonable prices. You'll also find bargain clothes for sale at markets and on push-carts.

Tailoring: Local tailors are experts when it comes to producing custom-tailored garments for both men and women, and are also adept at copying patterns. The result can be a suit of quality at a fair price—but made-to-measure clothing is not cheap.

Tea: Shops all over town, doling out tea leaves to enthusiastic local customers, will sell you gift tins of exotic blends.

Watches: The saying "Time is money" is quite literally true in Hong Kong: more is spent on watches and clocks here than on cameras and optical goods. Though most duty-free havens have watch bargains, in Hong Kong there is the advantage of an enormous variety of makes and models: Swiss, Japanese, American, luxury, or utilitarian styles are all on sale. However, be warned: Don't buy from a street-corner tout, and be sure to get the manufacturer's guarantee duly stamped or signed.

Woks and any other gadgets essential for Chinese cookery make good purchases. Department stores sell all sorts of intriguing kitchen equipment.

SPORTS

Watersports

In subtropical Hong Kong you can swim from April to early November. More than 30 "official" beaches—those patrolled by life-guards and with at least basic facilities—are found on the south and east coasts of Hong Kong island, in the New Territories and on three offshore islands. There are also many isolated beaches reachable only by boat. On summer weekends the "official" beaches do become extremely overpopulated, but the crowds are much less oppressive on weekdays and at the beginning and end of the season.

If Repulse Bay or the New Territories are too far away, try the public pools in Victoria Park or Kowloon Tsai Park.

Make the most of Hong Kong's sub-tropical climate with a dip at Kowloon's Tsai Park.

Diving: The coral and tropical fish in Hong Kong's waters are best seen far from the centres of population. For information and advance planning on how to get to the best diving areas, contact the Hong Kong Underwater Federation, GPO Box 9012, Hong Kong, tel. 25 04 81 54, or YMCA Scuba Club, c/o YMCA, Salisbury Road, Kowloon, Hong Kong. For last-minute arrangements, try the Sea Dragon Skin Diving Club, tel. 25 43 22 27.

Sailing: Because of the heavy harbour traffic, only sailors licensed by the Hong Kong authorities can run pleasure boats in local waters. However, it is possible to hire a crewed junk. Check with the tourist association for a list of yacht clubs.

Waterskiing: A boat, with operator and skis included, can be hired from the Hong Kong Waterski Club, tel. 81 20 391. The club is at the beach just northwest of Repulse Bay.

Sports Ashore

Golf: Some large hotels can arrange guest privileges at one of the Royal Hong Kong Golf Club's three 18-hole courses at Fanling in the New Territories, or the 9-hole course at Deep Water Bay, or at the Discovery Bay Golf Club on Lantau island. The Hong Kong Tourist Association also organizes a "Sports and Recreation" tour to the private Clearwater Bay Golf and Country Club on the tranquil Sai Kung peninsula.

Hiking: Local hikers fan out every weekend through the New Territories, the larger islands, and Hong Kong island, where a network of paths discloses some surprisingly open and appealing scenery. Maps of hiking trails in the popular areas are available at the Government Publications Centre in Hong Kong's General Post Office. Also, the Hong Kong Tourist Association publishes guides to Lantau Island and the Sai Kung peninsula, which has two official country parks, together with a self-guided walking tour of the island of Cheung Chau.

A giant videoscreen dominates the Sha Tin racecourse.

Ice- and roller-skating: A big indoor ice rink is located at Lai Chi Kok Amusement Park and another in Hung Hom, in Kowloon; both types of skating are on offer at City Plaza, Taikoo Shing, Quarry Bay; Sha Tin's New Town Plaza in the New Territories has a roller rink and tenpin bowling alley.

Tennis: The public courts at Victoria Park, Kowloon Tsai Park, and Bowen Road are open every day; bookings are taken only for Saturdays and Sundays (a week in advance).

Spectator Sports

Horseracing: All levels of society share a feverish interest in the Sport of Kings. Hong Kong maintains two tracks—the traditional Happy Valley course on Hong Kong island and the striking Sha Tin establishment in the New Territories. From September to June the Hong Kong Tourist Association runs a "Come Horseracing Tour," which includes lunch or dinner at the Royal Hong Kong Jockey Club visitors' box as well as entry to the members' enclosure.

Cricket: This has moved from a pitch incongruously located in the shadow of the Communist Chinese bank to new quarters in Wong-Nei-Chong Gap Road. Across the harbour, the Kowloon Cricket Club plays at a ground in Cox's Road.

> Depending on its pronunciation the word *ma* can have several meanings, e.g. "mother," "hemp," "horse," or "to curse."

ENTERTAINMENT

By day or by night, the action never stops in this most vibrant of cities. If the choice of nightlife seems too bewildering, pick up a copy of Hong Kong Tourist Authority's *Dining and Entertainment Guide* for listings of traditional establishments, or just simply wander through the maze of neon signs and take your pick. Culture buffs are also well catered for, and there is always a varied programme of events ranging from world-class opera to local amateur dramatic productions. Highlights of the arts calendar are the annual Arts Festival held in February and the Hong Kong International Film Festival in April. For the latest news on current events, you can consult the HKTA's *Hong Kong Diary* or check the local newspapers.

Folklore

Chinese opera: To most foreigners, this unique art form is likely to be inscrutable even after a couple of exposures. Even so, everyone appreciates the glittering costumes and the clear difference between heroes and villains. Although the music may seem strange to the unaccustomed ear, it certainly won't put you to sleep; cymbals and drums guarantee your alertness.

Calendar of Festivals

For the most up-to-date information, consult the Hong Kong Tourist Authority, or pick up a free copy of the HKTA's *Hong Kong Diary*. Note that precise dates cannot be given as Chinese festivals are fixed according to the lunar calendar.

January/February: *Lunar New Year.* Everything in Hong Kong, even business, shuts down for about three days. A time for paying debts, dressing up, and giving gifts. The dominant motif for the holiday is flowers. People visit temples and hand out *lai see* (lucky money) packets to children and unmarried friends, accompanied by the words "Kung Hei Fat Cho" ("May you prosper in the New Year").

February: *Spring Lantern Festival* (Yuen Siu). The last day of the Chinese New Year celebrations. Also known as Chinese Valentine's Day, since it was traditionally the time when unmarried women donned their finest clothes and ventured out with their chaperones to meet some eligible young men.

April: *Ching Ming Festival.* This Confucian festival, timed to the solar calendar, is one of two annual holidays on which to honour the dead. Ancestors' graves are swept and offerings of food, wine, or flowers made, while gold and silver "money" is burned to give the ancestors enough to spend in the afterworld.

April/May: *Birthday of Tin Hau.* The Taoist Goddess of the Sea is honoured by fisherfolk with prayers for safe voyages and good catches. Liveliest celebration is at Joss House Bay, where decorated junks and sampans converge with offerings. Spectators can reach the beach by special excursion boats. Smaller-scale celebrations, including lion-dancing, take place at other Tin Hau temples, notably at Aberdeen.

May: *Birthday of the Lord Buddha.* In Buddhist temples throughout the territory, the Buddha's image is bathed in scented water to symbolize the washing away of sins. *Cheung Chau Bun Festival.* The small, unspoiled island of Cheung Chau celebrates its thanksgiving holiday over seven days with roots going back to pirate days. Processions, lion and dragon dances, Chinese opera, and traditional rites at the Pak Tai Temple give the island a carnival atmosphere.

May/June: *Dragon Boat Festival* (Tuen Ng). Said to commemorate the watery death of an ancient Chinese statesman-poet Qu Yuen. Oarsmen in long, thin dragon boats race to the beat of big bass drums and Chinese gongs. Annual International Dragon Boat races are usually held a few days after the festival in June or July.

July: *Birthday of Lu Pan.* The Taoist patron saint of carpenters and builders is honoured with celebratory banquets.

August: *Seven Sisters' (Maidens') Festival.* A festival for lovers centred on an ancient Chinese legend. Women praying for husbands leave offerings at Lovers' Rock. *Hungry Ghosts Festival* (Yue Lan). Paper offerings are burned and food left out to placate ghosts who have been temporarily released from the underworld.

September: *Mid-Autumn Festival.* Celebrating the year's harvest, this one is a children's favourite. As the full moon rise, tots carrying paper lanterns of traditional or space-age design congregate in open or high places to admire the poetic sight. They eat moon cakes (ground sesame and lotus seeds or dates, perhaps enriched with duck egg) and take full advantage of being allowed to stay up late.

October: *Cheung Yeung Festival.* Nineteen centuries ago, so it is said, a man visited the hills on the advice of a fortune-teller. When he returned he found he was the sole survivor of a calamity. On the ninth day of the ninth moon, people visit the hillside graves of their ancestors and try to reach some high place for luck.

Lion and dragon dances: Agile young men in symbolic lion costumes romp to the tune of gongs and drums. These dances may be a part of almost any festival, and are even used to enliven the proceedings at official ceremonies. The dragon dance requires squads of performers to climb beneath the flexible shape of a long, fierce dragon and animate it as they dance. If a dignitary is in attendance, he or she is invited to "dot the eyes" of the dragon's face with a brush, thereby giving symbolic life to the festive monster.

Puppet shows: Whether suspended on strings, elevated on rods, worn as gloves, or cast as shadows on a screen, Chinese puppets and marionettes often reproduce the conventions of the old-fashioned operas. All types of puppet show, delighting children and adults alike, may be found offered free at public parks and playgrounds.

Arts and Culture

Festivals

Hong Kong Arts Festival: Every February the territory absorbs a dose of culture with concerts, recitals, plays, jazz, Chinese opera, and other productions put on by leading talents from both East and West. Tickets for the shows must be reserved well in advance.

Festival of Asian Arts: For two weeks every other October Hong Kong plays host to orchestras and dance, opera, and drama companies from all over Asia. There are also supplementary, free performances held in the open air.

Hong Kong International Film Festival: During the festival in April, some of the best international films are shown at various venues. Ask at City Hall about advance bookings.

Music, Performing Arts

For much of the year the City Hall cultural complex, the Arts Centre, Hong Kong Academy for the Performing Arts, the Hong Kong Cultural Centre in Kowloon, and town halls in the New Territories keep up a steady output of recitals, concerts, and plays by both local and overseas artists. The Hong Kong Philharmonic Orchestra and the Hong Kong Chinese Orchestra both maintain a full concert schedule. Larger arenas, including the Queen Elizabeth Stadium, the Hong Kong Coliseum, and the Ko Shan Theatre in Kowloon play host to various pop concerts, sporting events, and variety shows.

Hong Kong's three professional dance companies—the Hong Kong Ballet Company, the Hong Kong Dance Company, and the City Contemporary Dance Company—perform regularly, and there are a number of combined

Paper lanterns greet the rising moon at the Mid-Autumn festival to celebrate the year's harvest.

Puppet shows often emulate the styles of Chinese Opera. These opera performers have the look of marionettes.

dinner/theatre productions held periodically at the Hong Kong Hilton. Experimental theatre is organized at the Fringe Club.

Nightlife

Hong Kong by night can suit any taste—riotous, sedate, raw, or cultured. You can dress up for a nightclub or dress down to watch a street-corner opera. A night out in Hong Kong can be as glamorous or as earthy as your mood.

Tours: Excursion firms offer several different nightlife tours sampling the more elegant entertainment venues. The tours are handy and quite suitable for all visitors, including unaccompanied women, who might otherwise feel ill at ease on the nightclub circuit. As the package is paid for in advance, no one need worry about unexpected budgetary bombshells. Some tours combine a Chinese banquet and a gala show, perhaps adding a visit to an open-air market and the panorama from Victoria Peak. A different variation includes dinner and dancing on board an air-conditioned floating nightclub.

Nightclubs: Situated in the principal hotels, Hong Kong's most distinguished nightclubs have bands, dancing, and floor shows, some of which feature international stars. Other hotels, and many a nearby basement, also have discos where the lights keep flashing from 10:00 P.M. well into the early hours of the morning.

Pubs and bars: There is a vast range of watering holes to choose from in Hong Kong, from a luxurious lounge to a seedy bar. For a quiet drink or a snack with some background music and a non-girlie-bar atmosphere, several British- or Australian-style pubs are to be found. "Happy hour," when prices for standard drinks are reduced, is generally between 5:00 and 8:00 P.M.

Japanese karaoke bars have now become extremely popular with the locals. Night after night hoardes of people converge on these sing-along entertainment lounges and mime to the latest hits in front of a duly appreciative audience.

Hostess clubs: The Japanese tourist influx has inspired a growth of nightspots in which hostesses chat with the clients at a standard hourly rate. With the cover charge and the price of the drinks, these nightspots are exclusively for those who are not on a budget.

Cinemas: There are more than 30 cinemas in Hong Kong, and the latest Western releases are shown in some of the larger ones. Regular showings take place throughout the day, with a midnight showing at the weekend (which usually starts around 11:40 P.M.) Seats may be booked in advance. Language problems do arise, however; although the English-language films have Chinese subtitles, the films with Mandarin dialogue require both English and Chinese subtitles (for the benefit of the Cantonese-speaking Hong Kong audiences).

CHILDREN'S HONG KONG

There is no shortage of opportunities for children to have fun in Hong Kong, and visitors who have youngsters to entertain will find a wealth of attractions to choose from.

Entertainment on an aquatic theme at Ocean Park is popular with children of all ages. There's a special Kid's World, which those under 12 can enter free when accompanied by a paying adult. The shark aquarium and Wave Cove won't fail to appeal, while the more daring can try out the terrifying roller-coaster rides. Just next door, you'll find Water World, which is open from April to October and provides yet more water-based fun and games.

The period costumes and meticulous reconstructions of bygone China at Sung Dynasty Village and Middle Kingdom are fascinating for older children. Demonstrations of the ancient crafts of silk weaving, paper manufacture, and incense making are educational as well as delightful to watch.

The Hong Kong Tourist Authority offers an evening tour of Sung Dynasty Village, with exhilarating open-air performances of Chinese folk dance and acrobatics.

Hong Kong's museums are not just for adults. The Science Museum in Tsimshatsui East allows children to get their hands on over half of its 500 exhibits, while the nearby Space Museum has regular screenings on an enormous Omnimax screen in its Space Theatre, making the night sky come vibrantly alive.

For children who love boats, an inexpensive treat is an evening ride across the harbour on the Star Ferry, or simply watching the colourful chaos of junks and sampans bobbing on the water. Longer ferry trips to the outlying islands will also appeal. On the island of Cheung Chau is a legendary pirate's lair: Cheung Po Tsai cave is said to conceal buried treasure.

Hong Kong's trams and funicular will provide a thrill for many children, and a journey up Victoria Peak on the Peak Tram to look out over Victoria Harbour will appeal.

Innumerable shops selling toys and electronic games for children can be found all over Hong Kong, which may please parents less than it does their children. More traditional toys can be found in the Chinese-product department stores.

If you plan to visit during May, the carnival atmosphere of the Cheung Chau Bun Festival, with its high bamboo-and-paper towers, as high as 16 metres (54 feet) and covered in sticky buns, will fascinate the young ones (see page 79), while the Mid-Autumn Festival in September provides children with the perfect excuse to stay up late and watch magical candle-lit processions.

Feeding the Koi carp outside the Bank of China building — one of Hong Kong's tallest structures.

EATING OUT

The Chinese care about food with a passion only the French begin to rival. In Hong Kong, the chefs have a demanding clientele, and they use the best ingredients—fresh from local farms and the sea. You would have to search high and low to find a bad Chinese meal here.

The big problem is how to choose among the thousands of restaurants. Menus are not normally posted outside, so a certain amount of guesswork is involved. However, you can get an idea from a restaurant's windows, which may display live fish in tanks, or dressed poultry hanging from hooks.

About 50,000 ideograms exist in Chinese, of which 5,000 or so are in common use.

Even in the Chinese equivalent of a local café there may be hundreds of items on the menu. Let the waiter help you to choose just the right amount of food with the best range of tastes and textures. The more people in your party the better, since everyone shares all the dishes, increasing the opportunities for discovery.

Chinese food comes in half a dozen principal styles, all very different from one another. In Hong Kong you'll also find restaurants offering other Asian cuisines, and Western-style steak, pizza, vegetarian cuisine, and kosher food.

Meal Times

Hotels serve American, British, or continental breakfast from about 7:00 to 10:00 A.M.. At lunchtime business people pack the hotel restaurants from 1:00 to 3:00 P.M., guests dine between 7:30 and 9:30 P.M. The Chinese restaurants are more flexible; many open from breakfast until midnight or later without a break.

A traditional Chinese breakfast consists of *congee*, a rice gruel or porridge to which almost anything may be added, from fried batter to salted fish. At back-street breakfast stalls you'll also see the early risers digging into noodle soup with hunks of vegetable or pork.

EATING TRADITIONS

Dim Sum

Late breakfast or lunch can consist of tea and *dim sum*, the small snacks which add up to a delicious, filling meal. Servers wander from table to table chanting the Cantonese names of the foods contained in bamboo steamers on their trays or carts. Choose whatever looks interesting—from spring rolls, spare ribs, dumplings, and so on. Dozens of different delicacies are on show: from *siu mai* (pork and shrimp dumplings), to *har gau* (delicate steamed shrimp dumplings) and *cha siu bau* (barbecued pork buns). The constant comings and goings of clients, tea-waiters, and *dim sum* distributors tend to create a rather bazaar-like atmosphere, so prepare for an exciting, rather than relaxing, lunch. When you ask for the bill, the waiter will compute it on the basis of the number of empty dishes on the table. Unless you accidentally ordered a rare delicacy, you'll be happily surprised at the low total price.

Floating Food

Another novel eating experience is lunch or dinner afloat. Aboard the big floating restaurants found in Aberdeen, a delicious meal of fresh seafood is enhanced by the general nautical atmosphere.

An even more adventurous way of dining at sea can take place on any fine evening. If you hire a sampan from the Causeway Bay Typhoon Shelter you can be rowed out to a

The authentic taste of China's six main regional cuisines can be found in Hong Kong's restaurants.

fleet of floating kitchens which offer to cook you their specialities on the spot.

Food and the Chinese

For the Chinese, eating is a pleasure imbued with philosophical profundities: even the dead are offered food and wine to make their journey from this life more peaceful.

Perhaps food is so greatly valued because of memories of hard times in the past. The common Cantonese greeting is *"Nei sik jo fan mai a?"*—("Have you had your rice yet?"). In eras of hunger the Chinese learned to make the most of foods that might otherwise have seemed inedible—such as serpents, bizarre fish, and even the lining from swallows' nests.

> It is a custom to bring the bowl up to your mouth when eating with chopsticks.

Chinese gourmets demand the best flavours as well as other subtle factors which enhance the pleasure of the food—colour, texture, and presentation. So a proper Chinese meal is orchestrated—and must contain a harmonious progression from the sweet to the sour, the crunchy to the tender, the yellow of the pineapple to the red of the pepper. A Chinese banquet is a triumph of the well-rounded art of food.

Regional Cuisines

In a country as big as China regional styles of cooking were bound to develop. In Hong Kong restaurants every major school of Chinese cooking is represented, as establishments have inherited recipes and brilliant cooks from all parts of China. As most of Hong Kong's residents have roots just over the border in Guangzhou (Canton), the restaurants are mainly Cantonese. (They do not describe themselves as Cantonese, in the same way that a French restaurant situated in Paris would not advertise its nationality.)

A trip to one of Aberdeen's floating restaurants combines a boat trip and a delicious meal.

Cantonese

For visitors, this is probably the most familiar Chinese cuisine, as many Cantonese have emigrated, opened restaurants, and introduced new tastes to diners in the West. Be ready, though, for new sensations in Hong Kong, where the cooks have the authentic ingredients.

Steaming or stir-frying captures the natural flavour—as well as the colour and vitamins—in Cantonese food. A vast range of ingredients is used, and the flavours are many and often delicately understated.

Garoupa with ginger and spring onion: a popular, meat-flavoured, local fish steamed in the company of ginger, spring onions, and soya sauce, with a touch of garlic.

Sweet and sour prawns: shelled prawns in a sauce of sugar, vinegar, soya, and ketchup, coloured with the addition of crisp red and green peppers and pineapple chunks.

Lemon chicken: fried chunks of tender chicken in a creamy sauce of sugared lemon juice and chicken broth.

Crabmeat and corn soup: morsels of crab and kernels of maize in a thick, hearty soup. The Chinese usually have soup towards the end of the meal, but no one will be shocked if you want to begin with it.

Steamed white rice is normally served with a Cantonese meal, although you can order fried rice instead.

Chiu Chow

This cuisine from the Swatow region of southeast China excels in novel seasonings and rich sauces.

Minced pigeon: the pigeon meat is minced and fried with herbs, and you eat it wrapped in lettuce leaves. In Chiu Chow restaurants *congee* (rice porridge) is often served instead of steamed rice. Before and after dinner you will be presented with tiny cups containing a strong and bitter tea, known as Iron Buddha.

Hakka

The name Hakka means "guest people," referring to their migration to this region from northern China many centuries ago. Hakka cuisine involves the use of simple ingredients, especially versatile bean curd. Look for an ingenious dish called salted chicken; a coating of salt contains and increases the flavours while the bird is being baked.

Peking

The Chinese emperors made Beijing (Peking) the gourmet centre of the country, and Hong Kong's Peking restaurants still present truly Imperial banquets (ordered in advance) with everything from nuts to soup, in that order. You won't want to miss out on one of the world's most delicious eating experiences, Peking Duck. The duck is honey-coated before roasting, and is cut at the table. The celebrants put chunks of

Don't worry about the chopsticks — after a little practice you'll be quite an expert with them.

the crisp skin and tender flesh, along with spring onions and a sweet sauce, onto delicate pancakes, which are then rolled up and devoured.

Another Peking speciality is hot-sour soup, a peppery bracer of shredded pork and bamboo shoots, bean curd, spring onion, and mushrooms.

Wheat, not rice, is the staple food in northern China. Peking restaurants serve noodles and various kinds of bread. They also specialize in wonderful dumplings, stuffed with meat or vegetables and prepared by steaming or frying.

Shanghai

Both Peking and Shanghai restaurants serve a clever and delicious dish known as Beggar's Chicken. According to legend, the inventor was a tramp who stole a chicken but had no way to cook it. After tossing in some salt and onion, he smeared the bird in mud, then roasted it in his fire. When the mud was baked dry he smashed the coating. The feathers came off with the clay and all the juicy tenderness of the bird remained.

Peking and Shanghai restaurants usually serve noodles, rather than rice, with the meal.

The recipe has become more sophisticated as mushrooms, pickled cabbage, shredded pork, bamboo shoots, and wine are added to the stuffing. The ceremony of cracking the clay to reveal the chicken (which these days is wrapped in lotus leaves) all adds to the sense of occasion.

Shanghai food is generally more complicated as well as more thoroughly cooked than, say, Cantonese. Chilli peppers, garlic, and ginger are used in moderation. Shanghai diners usually prefer noodles to rice.

Szechwan

This food from southwestern China produces such sharp, hot flavours that it first takes your breath away, then awakens your palate. Once the fiery shock of the garlicized peppers has subsided, you can distinguish the other many elements in unlikely coexistence—bitter, sweet, fruity, tart, and sour.

Smoked duck, Szechwan style, is marinated in rice wine, with ginger and an array of spices, then steamed before being smoked over a specially composed wood fire.

Deep-fried beef with vegetables is a dish in which the meat and most of the other ingredients—carrots, celery, peppers, garlic—are shredded and slowly fried over a low flame.

All Chinese foods are pleasing to the eye, but there are some Szechwan foods that appeal to the ear. "Thunder" dishes are topped with crisp rice, which sizzles and pops on contact with the other ingredients.

Other Foods

While you're in the neighbourhood, take the opportunity to try some of the other Asian cuisines. There are restaurants in Hong Kong offering all the region's main cooking styles—Indian, Indonesian, Japanese, Korean, Thai, Malaysian, Filipino, and Vietnamese. So, if you long for a

The famous "thousand-year eggs" are duck eggs buried in lime for 60 days, with a resulting cheese-like taste.

vast Indonesian *rijsttafel* or authentic Japanese *sushi* or Korean *kimchee*—or even a "33" beer imported from Ho Chi Minh City—you will find it all here.

If you have a hankering for non-Asian food, you won't starve either. Hong Kong has a wide choice of American and many European-style restaurants, including French, Italian, Greek, and Mexican. Even more popular with the locals are Hong Kong's fast-food outlets, in which you can buy the traditional hamburger.

There are several good vegetarian restaurants which serve Chinese food. A lot of locals, not just Buddhist monks, keep the places crowded.

Drinks

The Chinese having a dinner party at the table next to you are probably drinking Cognac with their meal. Hong Kong claims the world's highest per-capita consumption of brandy, possibly because of a vague belief that it has aphrodisiac qualities. European and Australian table wines are also available, but at prices ranging from the tolerable to the quite shocking.

Chopsticks: Have a Go

You'll lose face—and fun—if you don't learn to use chopsticks to eat your food in Hong Kong.

First settle the bottom stick firmly at the conjunction of the thumb and forefinger, balancing it against the first joint of the ring finger. The second stick pivots around the fulcrum made by the tip of the thumb and the inside of the forefinger. If the sticks were parallel they would be wide enough to pick up an ice-cube; more often they meet at an acute angle.

If it's any consolation, many Chinese don't feel quite at home with knife and fork.

Few visitors develop a taste for Chinese wines, which have a 4,000-year history. Some are too sweet, others too strong. Unlike the Chinese grape and rice wines, the wheat wines are notorious for their alcoholic power. *Mou Tai* is a breathtaking case in point.

Visiting beer-lovers have a wide range of choice. The locally brewed San Miguel is cheap and refreshing. Tsingtao beer from China, in big green bottles, has a hearty European taste. You'll also find some of the best beers of Asia and Europe on better menus.

The Chinese virtually revere tea. They have been drinking it for many centuries as a thirst-quencher, general reviver, and ceremonial beverage. Jasmine-scented green tea or fermented black tea are most often encountered in Hong Kong. Tea in China is drunk without sugar and it's well worth making the effort to learn to appreciate the drink's unorthodox taste. (The only exception to this rule is in some breakfast places which serve English tea with milk and sugar.)

Rounding off the beverage list are familiar soft drinks and delicious tropical fruit juices. Coffee is available, though it is mainly served in Western-style restaurants and snack bars.

Etiquette

Except for formal banquets the Chinese pay little attention to protocol; they slurp the soup and let bits of food drop on to the tablecloth. All the more reason for visitors not to feel self-conscious about their lack of chopstick technique. (However, one thing worth remembering is that you should never place your chopsticks across the rice bowl, but let them rest either on the holder provided or against a plate.)

Table napkins are not normally provided in a Chinese restaurant, but hot, damp face towels may be distributed at the beginning or end of a meal, or at both times.

If Chinese hosts invite you to a restaurant, put yourself in their hands; they will try to order according to their impression of your tastes. You must eat some of every dish to avoid giving offence. If you're invited to dine at a Chinese home, it is the highest honour. Be sure to bring a small gift.

To Help You Order...

Have you a table?	**Yau mo toi ah?**
I'd like a/an/some…	**Ngor seung yiu…**
The bill, please.	**Mai dan, m goi.**

beer	**bei jau**	meat	**yuk**
chopsticks	**fai ji**	menu	**chan pye**
cup	**bui**	rice	**faan**
dessert	**tim bun**	soup	**tong**
fish	**yue**	tea	**cha**
fruit	**sang gwo**	water	**sui**
glass	**bor lay bui**	wine	**jau**

You won't get a fortune cookie at the end of your meal, but you might see a fortune teller on the street in Hong Kong.

Visit one of the tea houses in Hong Kong to sample the many varieties offered.

...and Read the Menu

蟹肉豆腐羹	bean curd and crabmeat soup
麻婆豆腐	bean curd with pork in pepper sauce
合桃鷄丁	diced chicken with walnuts
腰果肉丁	diced pork with cashew nuts
干燒冬筍	fried bamboo shoots and cabbage
炒鱔糊	fried eel with soya sauce
清炒蝦仁	fried shrimps
青椒肉絲	fried sliced pork with green pepper
茱扒鮮菇	mushrooms with vegetables
辣子鷄丁	shredded chicken with green pepper
豉椒牛肉	sliced beef with green pepper and bean sauce
三絲湯	sliced chicken, abalone and prawn soup
紅燒魚片	sliced fish with brown sauce
糟溜黃魚	stewed yellow fish
咕嚕肉	sweet and sour pork
鷄油津白	Tientsin cabbage and asparagus

INDEX

HANDY TRAVEL TIPS

An A–Z Summary of Practical Information

A

ACCOMMODATION (See also the list of RECOMMENDED HOTELS starting on page 129 , and YOUTH HOSTELS on page 128)

Hong Kong has more than 35,000 hotel rooms, most of them in luxury or first-class hotels, which is bad news for the budget-conscious tourist. From time to time the influx of visitors exceeds the supply of space, mostly in October and November but occasionally in the spring as well. During these seasons advance bookings are essential, though reservations are strongly recommended at any time of year.

For visitors arriving without accommodation, the Hotel Reservation Centre at the airports can arrange a room at any of the hotels in Hong Kong, Kowloon or the New Territories affiliated to the Hong Kong Hotels Association; the service is provided free of charge and the desk is open from 7am to midnight.

Hong Kong hotels include all the major international chains known around the world for their comfort and service. Even the more modest hotels are usually air-conditioned and offer more than just the basic services. However, exceptionally cheap (and therefore very basic) accommodation may be found in the Mong Kok and Yau Ma Tei areas or in the many guest houses and hostels in Chung King Mansions, Nathan Road, Tsimshatsui. The announced rates for hotels cover the room price only; a 10 percent service charge and a 5 percent government tax are added to the bill at check-out time.

AIRPORTS

Hong Kong International Airport, one of Asia's busiest, has a prize location almost in the centre of the city – which makes for dramatic landings amidst the rooftops of Kowloon. The single runway projects into the harbour on reclaimed land. The new Chek Lapkok International Airport, on an islet off Lantau Island and connected to Hong Kong by road and rail links, begins operation in 1998 and is designed to handle 35 million passengers a year.

Arrival. Arriving passengers go through immigration and customs checks in modern, efficient surroundings. Beyond the baggage inspection area you will find a bank, money changers, the Hotel Reservation Centre desk, and an information office of the Hong Kong Tourist Authority.

There are several ways of getting into town from Hong Kong International and Chek Lapkok airports. Major hotels operate their own limousine services; look for the dispatcher at the sign identifying your hotel. (Most hotels add the fare to your account.) Alternatively you can take a taxi. You should be charged only what the meter reads — plus an additional fixed sum if you take toll crossings — and a charge for each piece of luggage placed in the boot (trunk).

Air-conditioned airport coaches link the airports with the principal hotel zones and operate every 15 to 20 minutes from 7am to midnight. From Hong Kong International "Airbus" A1 goes to the district of Tsimshatsui in Kowloon, A2 to Hong Kong Central, A3 to Causeway Bay, and A5 to Taikoo Shing on Hong Kong island. If you do not have the correct change for the fare, go to the nearby Airbus Service centre for coins.

Departure. Airport coaches pass by main hotels every 15 minutes, but limousines will come only if previously arranged by the hotel hall porter. Taxis might be difficult to find at rush hour. The Hong Kong Tourist Authority warns that in heavy traffic congestion, it can take up to an hour and a half to reach Hong Kong International from central Hong Kong and 45 minutes from Kowloon's hotel district, though the road and rail links provide quick access to Chek Lapkok.

Check-in time is two hours before the flight's listed departure. A departure tax is levied on adults and children over 12, and this is payable in Hong Kong dollars only.

While it is officially not obligatory to tip an airport porter, in practice HK$3–$5.50 per bag is expected.

C

CAR HIRE (See also DRIVING on pp.108)

International and local car rental agencies operate in Hong Kong with both drive-yourself and chauffeur-driven cars. They offer Japanese, European, and American models.

Major credit cards are accepted by many agencies; a deposit is asked for only if you pay cash. The minimum age required is 25 and you must have held a driving licence for at least two years.

In view of the problems of traffic and parking, most tourists stick to taxis and public transport.

CLIMATE and CLOTHING

The best season to visit Hong Kong is autumn when the temperature and humidity drop and days are clear and sunny. From December until late February you'll find the air moderately cool with the humidity still low (around 73%). In spring the humidity and temperature start rising, and from May to mid-September it's hot and wet, with most of the annual rainfall recorded during these months.

The following chart gives an idea of the average monthly temperatures in Hong Kong, and the number of rainy days per month:

	J	F	M	A	M	J	J	A	S	O	N	D
°C	15	15	18	22	25	28	28	28	27	25	21	17
°F	59	59	64	72	77	82	82	82	81	77	70	63
days of rain	6	8	11	12	16	21	19	17	14	8	6	5

Clothing. From May to September very lightweight clothing is called for, and a raincoat and umbrella might come in handy. In restaurants and hotels, beware of the air-conditioning, which can reduce the temperature to freezing. From late September to early December shirtsleeves and sweaters are appropriate, while in winter — from late December to February — warm suits and dresses are necessary and an overcoat may be advisable.

Informality is generally the rule. For sightseeing and shopping, virtually any fashion is appropriate, but shorts are out of place in business districts and in Chinese temples. Bring along comfortable shoes for the steep slopes of Hong Kong.

COMMUNICATIONS

Post Offices. As in the United States, the post office of Hong Kong deals only with parcels and letters. The local postal service is fast and efficient, with several collections every day of the week, including Sundays and most holidays. Very urgent airmail letters and parcels can be mailed from the airport. Postmen can read both Chinese and English addresses. Packages sent surface mail may take six to ten weeks to reach Europe or North America. Stamps are sold at post offices and hotels. Post boxes are red pillar boxes.

Telegrams. HK Telecommunications Limited runs Hong Kong's telecommunications links with the rest of the world. Hotels will normally send telegrams for their clients, or you can go to the HKT office at 10 Middle Road, Tsimshatsui, which is open 24 hours a day.

Faxes. Most post offices offer a telefax service, or you can use the facilities in the business centre at your hotel. Some of the larger hotels offer rooms with private fax lines.

Telephones. Hong Kong's telephone system for both local and international calls is excellent. You will find few phone booths or coin-operated telephones; if you do, they require a HK$1 coin. Most people simply pick up any telephone — in a bar or shop — and use it even without asking permission. Local calls cost the subscriber nothing in Hong Kong, hence the generosity of phone owners. Hotels may charge a handling fee for local calls.

For an English-speaking information service dial 1081; if you have difficulties in getting a number, dial 109. Information on phone locations and on the purchase and operation of stored-value cards and coin phones is available by dialling 013. Stored-value cards cost HK$50, $150, and $200 and are on sale at Hong Kong Tourist Authority centres.

For overseas calls dial 001 (010 for collect/reverse charge calls) to go to a HKT office. Direct dial overseas calls can be made from IDD public phone booths.

The international telephone country code for Hong Kong is 852.

COMPLAINTS

The Hong Kong Tourist Authority will mediate between visitors and shops and establishments which are members of the association. In cases of overcharging by taxi drivers, complaints should be addressed to the Traffic Complaints Office; dial 2527 7177. In other cases, complaints may be directed to:

The Consumer Council, 22/F, K Wah Centre, 191 Java Road, North Point, Hong Kong; tel. 2929 2222.

The Community Advice Bureau, 15B Right Emperor Commercial Building, 122-126 Wellington Street, Central, Hong Kong; tel. 2815 5444.

CRIME (See also EMERGENCIES on page 109, and POLICE on page 120)

As the signs in the trams warn you, "Beware of pickpockets." This applies to any crowded place, and Hong Kong has some of the most crowded places you've ever seen. Avoid carrying large amounts of cash and leave valuables in your hotel's safe deposit box. Otherwise, tourists have nothing special to fear and Hong Kong is generally considered safe by night and day. In case of emergencies, dial **999** and seek help from the police.

CUSTOMS and ENTRY FORMALITIES

All visitors must have a passport or other valid travel document. U.K. subjects are generally granted a twelve-month stay without a visa. Nationals of more than 50 other countries, including the U.S., Canada, Australia, and New Zealand, need no visas for visits of up to one month (three months in some cases). For longer visits a formal application has to be made. For further information, contact an office of the Hong Kong Tourist Authority (see page 123).

Though Hong Kong is a free port, excise duties are charged on alcohol and tobacco. Though import duties may change: as the Chinese continue to restructure the administration of the former colony (check with the Hong Kong Tourist Authority for updates), you can bring into Hong Kong duty-free: 200 cigarettes or 50 cigars or 250 grams tobacco, and 1 litre spirits or 1 litre wine. When returning home, the quotas you can import duty-free are as follows: **Australia** 200 cigarettes or 250 grams cigars or 250 grams tobacco, and 1 litre spirits or 1 litre wine; **Canada** 400 grams tobacco, and 1.4 litres spirits, and 1.4 litres wine; **N. Zealand** 200 cigarettes or 50 cigars or 250 grams tobacco, and 1.1 litres spirits and 4.5 litres wine; **S. Africa** 400 cigarettes and 50 cigars and 250 grams tobacco, and 1 litre spirits and 2 litres wine; **UK/Republic of Ireland** 200 cigarettes or 50 cigars or 250 grams tobacco, and 1 litre spirits and 2 litres wine; **U.S.** 200 cigarettes and 100 cigars and a reasonable quantity of tobacco, and 1 litre spirits, or 1 litre wine.

Hong Kong

Firearms must be declared and surrendered into official custody until the visitor leaves Hong Kong. A reasonable quantity of perfume (in opened bottles) may be brought in, and there are no currency restrictions in either direction.

D

DRIVING

Anyone over 18 with a valid licence and third-party insurance can drive in Hong Kong for 12 months without having to pay for a local licence. Road blocks designed to keep illegal immigration in check are very common in Hong Kong and drivers must carry a valid driving licence and photo identification at all times.

Driving conditions. As in Britain and Australia, Hong Kong traffic keeps to the left. Congestion is a serious problem, sometimes leading to impatient, imprudent driving. Beware of inattentive pedestrians. Speed limit: 30mph (50km/h) in towns, elsewhere as marked.

Parking. This can be a headache, especially in central areas, despite the multi-storey car-parks. In busy streets the meters operate from 8am to midnight Monday to Saturday, and wardens are ever alert. There are plans for Sunday and holiday parking meters to be introduced in some districts.

Breakdowns. Telephone the firm from which you rented the car. In an emergency, dial 999 for the police.

Road signs . Most road signs in Hong Kong are the standard international pictographs.

The following words may help you in explaining your problems to non-English-speaking Chinese:

There's been an accident.	**Yau yi ngoi a.**
collision	**jong che**
flat tire	**tire baau tai**

E

ELECTRIC CURRENT

Standard voltage in Hong Kong is 200/220-volt, 50-cycle AC. Many hotels have razor fittings for standard plugs and voltages. Elsewhere, sockets come in many sizes. American irons need special adapters.

EMBASSIES and CONSULATES

For complete lists of consulates, look in the classified directory (*Yellow Pages*) for Hong Kong island — under Consulates or, for Commonwealth countries, under Commissioners.

Generally speaking, the opening hours are 9am to noon and 2-5pm Monday to Friday. To make absolutely sure, telephone first.

Australia: 23rd-24th floors, Harbour Centre, 25 Harbour Road, Hong Kong; tel. 2827 8881.

Canada: 11th-14th floors, Tower 1, Exchange Square, Hong Kong; tel. 2810 43 21.

New Zealand: 34th floor, Jardine House, Connaught Road Central, Hong Kong; tel. 2877 4488.

South Africa: 27th floor, Sunning Plaza, 10 Hysan Avenue, Causeway Bay, Hong Kong; tel. 2577 3279.

U.K.: British trade commission,visa section,3rd floor, 1 Supreme Court road, Hong Kong; tel. 2901 3111.

U.S.A.: 26 Garden Road, Hong Kong; tel. 2523 9011.

EMERGENCIES

Dial **999** and ask for the Police, Fire, or Ambulance department. A free St. John's ambulance service is obtainable by dialling 2576 6555 (Hong Kong island), or 2713 5555 (Kowloon), or 2639 2555 (New Territories).

The main hospitals treat urgent medical problems 24 hours a day in their emergency wards, and hotels often have doctors on call.

Queen Mary Hospital, Pok Fu Lam Road, Hong Kong; tel. 2855 4111.

Hong Kong

Queen Elizabeth Hospital, 30 Gascoigne Road, Kowloon; tel. 2710 2111.

Prince of Wales Hospital, 30-32 Ngan Shing Street, Sha Tin; tel. 2632 2211.

Round-the-clock service for dental emergencies is found at: The Adventist Hospital, 40 Stubbs Road, Hong Kong; tel. 2574 6211.

The Yellow Pages of the telephone directory has listings under Physicians and Surgeons and Dental Practitioners.

| Help! | **Gau meng ah!** |
| Police! | **Geng tsa!** |

ETIQUETTE

In the rush and hubbub of Hong Kong a smile goes a long way. But don't be disappointed if the reaction seems cool. The Chinese are not demonstrative and may be flustered by those who are. Always use formal terms of address (e.g., Mr. Wong) until invited to do otherwise. The Chinese put their family name first, followed by the given name, then the middle name.

Business cards are frequently exchanged in Hong Kong. You should hold out your card with both hands when presenting it to a Chinese person. If you are offering a gift, make sure you choose carefully; avoid objects considered unlucky, such as clocks, anything coloured white, black, or blue, or sharp implements. When presenting flowers, the number should be even.

F

FERRIES and BOAT EXCURSIONS

Private tourism companies run many different harbour and island excursions with guides and refreshments. Their flamboyant ferries and modified junks dock near Star Ferry (in Kowloon and Hong Kong). Some of their programmes consist of combination tram and ferry rides, often ending with a splendid Chinese meal on board.

You can go to Macau either by jetfoil or hoverferry. The journey takes about an hour. Alternatively, you may prefer the luxurious high-speed ferries. Somewhat slower than the above, but considerably faster than conventional ferryboats, they make the crossing in about 90 minutes.

G

GUANGZHOU

Banks and currency exchange. Foreign currency and traveller's cheques may be exchanged in hotels and Friendship Stores. Take your passport along. Keep the receipt in case you want to change excess money back to foreign currency when leaving the country.

Currency. Chinese "people's money," called *renminbi* (RMB), is based on the *yuan*, divided into 100 *fen*. Ten *fen* make a *jiao*. The two-tier currency scheme has been abolished and Foreign Exchange Certificates (FEC) no longer exist. Friendship Stores, hotels, and all other establishments now accept only RMB.

Customs. China sets liberal quotas on the amount of cigarettes, wine, and film you can bring with you, but restrictions affect reading matter, radio transmitters, weapons etc. Ask for the latest regulations when you apply for your visa.

Driving. Unlike Hong Kong, the rest of China drives on the right. Self-drive cars are not available for rental.

Electric current. 220-volt, 50-cycle AC.

Getting there. Several daily flights link Hong Kong and Guangzhou. Train travellers can cover the distance in less than three hours aboard deluxe expresses. Another way of travelling is the regular hovercraft service from Tai Kok Tsui (Kowloon) to the port of Whampoa.

Language. Though Cantonese is the local dialect (as in Hong Kong), a substantial proportion of the people speak the national language, putonghua (known abroad as Mandarin). Hotel staff know some English.

Photography. It is forbidden to film military objects, soldiers, industrial establishments, etc.

Public transport. Buses and trolley-buses cover the major routes. Tourists are more likely to use taxis, which are best ordered through the hotel.

Restaurants. Note that dinner hours are earlier than in many countries, 6 to 7:30pm on average.

Hong Kong

Shopping hours. Usually from 9am to 7pm, seven days a week.

Tipping. Not permitted. But a small gift to, say, a tour guide would not be out of place.

Tourist information offices. For information on travel to China, consult a Chinese embassy or consulate or one of the following:

United Kingdom: China Tourist Office, 4 Glentworth Street, London NW1.

USA: China International Travel Service, 60 E. 42nd Street, New York, NY 10165.

Hong Kong: China International Travel Service, South Sea Centre, 75 Mody Road, Tsimshatsui East; tel. 2732 5888, or China Travel Service (HK) Ltd, 77 Queens Road, Central; tel. 2522 0450.

Visas. Certain approved travel agents as well as China International Travel Service expedite matters in as little as 24 hours.

Water. You should avoid tap water everywhere in mainland China. However, you can safely drink the boiled (for tea making) water in hotel-room thermos flasks.

GUIDES and TOURS

Several private companies run guided tours of Hong Kong, the New Territories, and the islands. See Sightseeing Tours or Travel Bureaux in the Yellow Pages of the telephone directory.

The Hong Kong Tourist Authority organizes a huge assortment of tours, ranging from a half-day tour of Hong Kong island to tours of the harbour and further afield to the New Territories, Lantau and Cheung Chau islands, Macau, Shenzhen, and Guangzhou. For full details, ask at your hotel or one of the HKTA's information centres.

L

LANGUAGE (see also the inside front cover and page 128)

The official languages of Hong Kong are English and Mandarin Chinese; Cantonese is commonly spoken by the local residents. (Though Chinese dialects may vary from one another considerably in pronunciation, the characters are the same.) English is understood in most situations. The following approximations of Cantonese greetings may help you make contact with the locals:

Good morning	**jo san**
Good afternoon	**ng on**
Good evening	**mang on**
Good night	**jo tau**
Goodbye	**joy geen**
Please (for service)	**m goi**
Please (invitation)	**tcheng**
Thank you (for service)	**m goi**
Thank you (for a gift)	**dor jeh**

Here are some everyday Hong Kong words:

amah	housemaid
chop	seal or stamp on a document
fung shui	lucky siting of building or graves
gwailo	Europeans, foreigners
hong	big business firm
joss	luck
pak pai	illegal taxi
yam seng	"cheers," "bottoms up"

LAUNDRY and DRY-CLEANING

In many hotels laundry and dry-cleaning are routinely returned the same day. Of course, prices are much higher than in neighbourhood establishments. For addresses off the tourist track, look in the Yellow Pages of the telephone directory under Cleaners and Dyers. Hong Kong also has a number of launderettes, where you can wash, spin, and dry your own load of clothing for a moderate price. Look in the Yellow Pages under Launderers — self service.

LOST PROPERTY

Check first with your hotel receptionist if you lose anything, then report the loss to the nearest police station or one of the "reporting centre" sub-stations found in busy areas.

MACAU

Currency. Macau's own currency, the pataca, is divided into 100 avos. The pataca (usually abbreviated $) is worth about the same as the Hong Kong dollar, which is also used as standard currency in Macau. Banks, hotels, money-changing offices, and casinos change traveller's cheques and foreign currency. There are no restrictions on import or export of money.

Customs. Passengers from Macau may return to Hong Kong with one duty-free bottle of wine and 200 cigarettes or 25 cigars.

Electric current. Hotels usually provide 220-volt, 50 cycle power, but some areas of Macau are still on 110 volts.

Emergency. Dial **3333** for police, **2222** for fire.

Getting there. Jetfoil, hovercraft, high-speed ferry, and conventional ferryboat services are frequent between Hong Kong and Macau, but advance reservations are advisable — you can book at the ticket office in Mong Kok MTR station or at the Hong Kong–Macau Ferry Terminal, 200 Connaught Road West. Macau's new airport, opened in 1995, handles flights to and from Hong Kong, mainland China, Taiwan, and many other international destinations.

Languages. Cantonese is most people's mother tongue, and English is more widely known than Macau's official language, Portuguese, which is mainly used in government bureaus, courts, etc.

Mini-mokes. These Jeep-like vehicles can be hired at the Macau Ferry Terminal. Bring a valid driving licence or an International Driving Permit.

Pedicabs. Used by locals as well as tourists, these bike-propelled taxis have no meters, so it's best to agree on the price in advance. Visitors often take a tour at an hourly rate.

Post office. Macau postage stamps may by bought at the main post office or in hotels. The red pillar-boxes are marked *Correio*.

Public transport. Several bus routes cover the city as well as the islands. Take the topless yellow double-decker bus to Coloane for sightseeing on the way. Bus stops are marked by a red disc reading *Paragem autoomnibus*.

Taxis. Metered taxis are abundantly available except at holiday time.

Tourist information offices.

Australia: Macau Government Tourist Office, 449 Darling Street, Balmain, NSW 2041; tel. (02) 555 7548.

U.K.: Macau Government Tourist Office, 1 Battersea Church Road, London SW11 3LY; tel. (0171) 771 7059.

U.S. and Canada: Macau Government Tourist Office, P.O. Box 350; Kennilworth, IL 60043; tel. (847) 751 6421 or (800) 331 7150.

Hong Kong: Macau Government Tourist Office, 3704 Shun Tak Centre, 200 Connaught Road Central; tel. 2540 8180. There's also an information desk at Hong Kong Airport.

In Macau itself: Department of Tourism and Information, Edificio Ritz, Largo do Senado 11, Macau; tel. (853) 315 566.

Visas. Visitors from most West European countries (including Great Britain) as well as Australia, Canada, the U.S., New Zealand, Japan, and the Philippines are admitted to Macau visa-free. Most others are granted visas automatically on arrival by showing a valid passport and paying the fee. But if your country maintains no diplomatic relations with Portugal, you must apply for a visa in advance from a Portuguese consulate overseas.

When to go. The best climate is spring and autumn. Avoid Chinese New Year and the November Grand Prix when Macau is jammed.

MAPS

The Hong Kong Tourist Authority has excellent free maps covering the principal commercial areas of Hong Kong and Kowloon. They also sell various other maps and street directories, as do leading bookstores. Maps meeting almost any need are sold at the Map Sales Office, 10th Floor, Kowloon Government Offices, 405 Nathan Road, Kowloon (tel. 2780 0981) and at the Government Publications Centre, 66 Queensway.

Hong Kong

MEDIA

Newspapers and Magazines. Hong Kong has more than 100 news-papers in the Chinese language. The three most popular English-language dailies are the *South China Morning Post*, the *Eastern Express*, and the *Hong Kong Standard*. The *Asian Wall Street Journal*, published Monday to Friday in Hong Kong, emphasizes business and financial coverage. The *International Herald Tribune*, edited in Paris, is printed simultaneously in Hong Kong six days a week. Newspapers and magazines from Europe, Asia, and the U.S. are sold at hotel bookstalls and leading bookshops.

Useful tourist publications produced by the Hong Kong Tourist Authority are the weekly *Hong Kong This Week*, which contains information on current events, a shopping guide, and useful tips on where to eat and how to get around town, and the weekly listings magazine *Hong Kong Diary*.

Radio and Television. Hong Kong has two TV channels in English and two in Chinese. The Chinese channels sometimes show foreign-language films which are dubbed into Cantonese; satellite and cable stations are becoming increasingly available.

There are six English-language radio channels providing a broad range of programmes, from easy listening to news and current affairs. The BBC World Service also broadcasts 24 hours a day.

MEDICAL CARE (See also EMERGENCIES on page 109)

Since health care can be expensive, it is advisable to consult your insurance company at home for information on policies covering illness or accident on holiday.

Requirements for vaccinations change from time to time so be sure to check with your travel agent or airline before departure. At last report Hong Kong had dispensed with the requirement for smallpox or cholera vaccination, except for passengers arriving from infected areas. Macau normally follows suit. Since requirements can change without notice, it is best to check with your travel agent or the tourist office before departure.

Malaria has made a comeback in recent years in Southeast Asia. Fansidar, a drug available without prescription in Hong Kong, is an effective safeguard against the mosquito-borne disease.

Hong Kong has up-to-date hospitals on both sides of the harbour. For minor ailments, chemists (druggists) can often recommend and supply certain medicines, but it will not be possible for you to get a foreign prescription filled.

Many local pharmacies adhere to both Western and Eastern concepts of health care, displaying familiar pills and bottles along with exotic herbs, roots, dried seahorses, and powdered antlers.

I want to see a…	**Ngor yiu tai…**
doctor	**yee sang**
dentist	**nga yee**

MONEY MATTERS

Currency. Hong Kong's freely convertible currency, the Hong Kong dollar (abbreviated $ or HK$), is divided into 100 cents (abbreviated ¢). Banknotes are circulated in denominations of 10, 20, 50, 100, 500, and 1,000 dollars. They are issued by two local banks, not by the Hong Kong government, which does, however, mint the coins. These come in denominations of 10, 20, and 50 cents and 1, 2, 5, and 10 dollars. Note that the 10-cent and 50-cent pieces look confusingly alike. There is a new HK$10 coin.

Currency exchange. Most foreign currencies can be changed at banks, hotels, money changers, and major shopping outlets. Independent money changers are legally obliged to display net exchange rates and to issue a note detailing the transaction for customers to sign in advance. If you plan to make a large foreign-currency transaction it's worthwhile shopping around, as exchange rates vary from place to place and day to day; check the current rates in the local newspaper. Both foreign and local banks have branches all over the territory, including small towns.

Traveller's cheques. Traveller's cheques are widely accepted in shops, though you'll probably get a better exchange rate at a bank. You must show your passport when you cash a cheque.

Credit cards. Major hotels, restaurants, and shops accept the well-known charge cards. Even the Chinese product department stores recognize certain credit cards.

Hong Kong

PLANNING YOUR BUDGET

Except for Chinese food, few big bargains brighten daily life in Hong Kong. However, for the tourist, shopping remains one of the great attractions and real bargains can be found in cameras and audio equipment, jewellery, some tailoring, and products from across the border in China. Bargain-hunters must be prepared to leave the tourist-orientated areas of Hong Kong island and Tsimshatsui to find low prices.

To give you an idea of what to expect, here are some average prices in Hong Kong dollars. However, they must be regarded as approximate; inflation is a factor in Hong Kong as elsewhere.

Airport. From Hong Kong International Airport via Airbus to Tsimshatsui HK$12.30, to Hong Kong island (Central, Causeway Bay, Taikoo Shing, or Kowloon Tong KCR station) HK$19. Taxi to Kowloon HK$50; to Hong Kong island HK$120-$150. From Chek Lapok, check with the Hong Kong Tourist Authority personel in the arrivals halls. Airport departure tax HK$100 for adults and children over 12.

Buses and trams. Buses HK$1–$32, trams HK$1.20 for adults, HK80¢ for children, minibuses HK$3-$10, maxicabs HK$1-$8, Peak Tram HK$14 (one way), HK$21 (return) for adults, HK$4 (one way), HK$6 (return) for children.

Car rental. Japanese models HK$690-$1,100 per day, HK$2,500-$4,500 per week, collision damage waiver HK$100 per day.

Cinema. HK$50-$60 (no reduction for children).

Ferries. Star Ferry HK$1.70-$2. Macau: ferry HK$86, high-speed ferry HK$120, hoverferry HK$110, jetfoil HK$132. Other islands HK$15-$30. Guangzhou (Canton): hovercraft HK$320 return (fares to Guangzhou increase during peak seasons such as Chinese New Year).

Hairdressers. Woman's haircut HK$200-$400, shampoo and blow-dry HK$150, permanent wave HK$600-$800.

Hotels. Hostels and guesthouses HK$150-$400, medium hotel HK$700 up, luxury hotel HK$1,200 and up. Add 10% service charge and 5% government tax.

Mass Transit Railway (single fare). Adults HK$3.50-$9, children HK$3-$4.

Meals and drinks. Set lunch HK$50-$120, dinner HK$120-$350, beer or soft drink HK$5-$15, carafe of wine HK$40 and up, spirits HK$30 and up.

Medical care. HK$150-$250 for a consultation.

Taxis. HK$14 for first 2 km (1.2 miles), HK$1 for each succeeding 200m, HK$20 for journeys via Cross Harbour Tunnel or Eastern Harbour Crossing (to cover driver's return toll), and HK$5 for each piece of baggage.

Trains. Kowloon to Lo Wu, first class HK$54, ordinary class HK$27.

OPENING HOURS

Most government offices are open 9am-1pm and 2-5pm Monday to Friday, and 9am-1pm Saturday.

Banks. Standard banking hours are 9am-4:30pm Monday to Friday, 9am-12:30pm Saturday. Money-changers' offices, found in most neighbourhoods, stay open much longer than banks. Even later you can change money at the airport or a hotel.

Post offices. The main post office on Hong Kong island is located next to the Star Ferry and is open 8am-6pm Monday to Friday, 8am-2pm Saturday. In Kowloon the main post office is between Jordan and Yau Ma MTR stations; open 9:30am-6pm Monday to Friday and 9:30am-1pm Saturday. All post offices are closed on Sunday and public holidays.

Shops. Major shops on Hong Kong island are open 10am-6pm, in Causeway Bay and Wanchai 10am-9:30pm, and in Kowloon 10am-7:30pm, although some stay open until 9pm. Most shops, apart from a few in Hong Kong Central, are open seven days a week.

Museums. Most museums close on public holidays like New Year's Eve, the Lunar New Year, etc. (see page 121 for list of public holidays).

Flagstaff House Museum of Tea Ware: 10am-5pm daily except Sundays.

Fung Ping Shan Museum: 10am-6pm daily except Thursdays and public holidays.

Hong Kong

Hong Kong Museum of Art: 10am-6pm daily except Mondays; 1-6pm Sundays and public holidays.

Hong Kong Museum of History: 10am-6pm daily except Mondays; 1-6pm Sundays and public holidays.

Hong Kong Space Museum: 2-9:30pm Monday to Friday, closed Tuesdays. Sky shows and natural history films in the Space Theatre hourly throughout the day beginning at 2:30pm (last show at 8:30pm). Saturday 1-9:30pm (first show 1:30pm, last 8:30pm). Sundays and public holidays 10:30am-9:30pm (first show at 11:30am, last 8:30pm). Shows are narrated in Cantonese, but a simultaneous translation is provided through headphones. One show a day is narrated in English (Sunday, Monday, Wednesday, Friday at 8:30pm; Thursday, Saturday at 6:30pm). To check times, tel. 2734 2722.

Lei Cheng Uk Museum: 10am-1pm and 2-6pm daily except Mondays; 1-6pm Sundays and public holidays.

Museu Luis de Camões, Macau: 11am-5pm daily except Wednesdays and public holidays.

Museum of Chinese Historical Relics: 10am-6pm daily.

Hong Kong Science Museum: 10am-9pm daily except weekends.

Sung Dynasty Village (Wax Museum): 11am-9pm daily.

P

PHOTOGRAPHY and VIDEO

Hong Kong is a good place to buy duty-free camera and video equipment, and to use it. Film is not expensive, and the processing is fast and reasonably priced. Make sure any video tapes you purchase are compatible with your equipment at home.

At the airport the luggage of departing passengers is X-rayed for security reasons. The best way of protecting films is to keep them in your hand luggage and remove them just before the inspection.

POLICE

The Hong Kong Police Force is one of the world's best equipped, with computerized and radio-controlled forces. It deals with crime, traffic, and even coast guard duties. Living up to Hong Kong's reputation as a fashion centre, the police dress in natty, trimly tailored uniforms. Those with a red label under their shoulder badges speak English, but all police are to some extent bilingual.

Where's the police station, please? **Tsai goon hai bean doe m goi?**

PUBLIC HOLIDAYS

Thanks to the convergence of British and Chinese traditions, Hong Kong celebrates 17 holidays a year. Though the banks close, most businesses carry on as usual. The only holiday on which Hong Kong really shuts down is the Lunar New Year. Chinese holidays are fixed according to the lunar calendar, so exact dates cannot always be given.

January 1	New Year's Day
January or February	Lunar New Year (3-4 days)
April	Ching Ming Festival
March or April	Good Friday
	The day following Good Friday
	Easter Monday
May or June	Tuen Ng (Dragon Boat) Festival
July	The first weekday in July
August	The first Monday in August
Last Monday in August	Liberation Day
September or October	The day following the mid-Autumn Festival
October	Chung Yeung Festival
December 25	Christmas Day
December 26	Boxing Day

R

RELIGION

Confucianism, Buddhism, and Taoism are the major religions in Hong Kong. The territory also has hundreds of Christian churches and chapels, the oldest being St. John's Cathedral (Church of England), built in the first decade of British rule. For details of services consult the telephone book's Yellow Pages under *Church Organiza-*

tions. The Saturday issue of the *South China Morning Post* runs announcements from churches.

Kowloon Mosque (Jamia Masjid) caters for Hong Kong's sizeable Muslim population. The Mosque and Islamic Centre are a short walk from the Star Ferry in Kowloon Park, off Nathan Road.

Hong Kong also has Hindu and Jewish houses of worship.

T

TIME DIFFERENCES

Before you make any overseas telephone calls, have a look at the following chart, lest you wake someone halfway round the world.

The hours refer to the months when many countries in the northern hemisphere move their clocks one hour ahead (Daylight Saving Time). Hong Kong stays the same year-round, at GMT + 8.

New York	London	**Hong Kong**	Sydney	Aukland
7am	noon	**7pm**	9pm	11pm

TIPPING

Most hotels and restaurants routinely add a 10 percent service charge, though an extra 5 percent may be given for especially good service.

Hairdresser/barber	10-20%
Lavatory attendant	HK$2–5
Maid, per week	HK$60
Hotel porter, per bag	HK$3–5
Taxi driver	10% (optional)
Tourist guide	10% (optional)
Waiter	5–10%

TOILETS

Public conveniences are not always easy to find except in the main tourist areas. Most are not well maintained, so conveniences located in a hotel or a fast-food restaurant may be a better bet.

Where are the toilets?　　　　**Chi saw hai bean doe?**

TOURIST INFORMATION

The Hong Kong Tourist Authority (HKTA) operates information and gift centres at key areas for visitors; the first one being in the arrival halls at the airports (open 8am-10:30pm daily, though subject to change). Leaflets and maps — and answers to questions — may also be obtained at the information and gift centre on the Star Ferry concourse, Tsimshatsui, Kowloon (open 8am-6pm Monday to Friday, 9am-5pm weekends and public holidays). The head office is at 9–11 F Citicorp Centre, 18 Whitfield Road, North Point, Hong Kong; tel. 2807 6543, fax 2806 0303 (open 9am-6pm Monday to Friday, 9am-1pm Saturday, closed Sunday and public holidays). The HKTA maintains site on the Internet at http://info @HTKA.org.

A telephone information service for visitors is available 8am-6pm Monday to Friday and 9am-5pm on Saturdays, Sundays and public holidays; dial 2807 6177.

Addresses of some overseas offices of the HKTA are as follows (for Guangzhou (Canton) see page 111, for Macau see page 114):

Australia: Level 4, Hong Kong House, 80 Druitt Street, Sydney, NSW 2000; tel. (02) 9283 3083.

Canada: Hong Kong Trade Centre, 9 Temperance Street, Toronto, Ontario M5H 1Y6; tel. (09) 575 2707.

New Zealand: PO Box 2120, Auckland; tel. (09) 521 3167.

South Africa: c/o Development Promotions (Pty) Ltd, PO Box 9874, Johannesburg 2000; tel. (011) 339 4865.

U.K.: 125 Pall Mall, London SW1Y 5EA; tel. (0171) 930 4775.

U.S.: Suite 2400, 610 Enterprise Drive, Oakbrook, IL 60521; tel. (630) 575 2828.

5th Floor, 590 Fifth Avenue, New York, NY 10036-4706; tel. (212) 869 5008/869 5009.

Suite 1220, 10940 Wilshire Boulevard, Los Angeles, CA 90024-3915; tel. (310) 208 4582.

TRANSPORT

Hong Kong's public transport system is one of the most efficient and varied in any capital city; it's also remarkably inexpensive. The new Octopus Card is similar to transit passes in other cities. You can purchase it in any amount and use it for transport on the MTR, KCR, ferries operated by HKF, and buses operated by KMB and Citybus.

Buses. The bus service in Hong Kong is good and relatively cheap. Double-decker buses run from 6am to 3am and cover even remote parts of Hong Kong. If you plan to do much sightseeing by bus, buy the timetable books issued by the Hong Kong island operator, China Motor Bus, and by the Kowloon Peninsula operator, Kowloon Motor Bus. Most bus stops are marked by a disc saying "all buses stop here." On most buses you must deposit the exact fare into the box next to the driver as you enter.

Minibuses. Hong Kong's "public light buses," seating 16 passengers, are fast and convenient. You can hail them everywhere and get off almost anywhere along their route. The destination is lit up above the front window in Chinese only on most buses, and in English as well on some others. Occasionally the fare is shown in Chinese numerals only. Pay the driver as you leave and keep a sufficient number of coins in your pocket, as it's not easy to get change.

Minibuses marked with a green stripe go to the Mid Levels, up to the Peak, and to Aberdeen. You can find them in Central. Minibuses marked with a red stripe have routes around West Point, Central, Causeway Bay, Quarry Bay, and Shau Kei Wan. Some of them also go over to Kowloon, and these minibuses can be hailed in Causeway Bay or Wanchai.

Maxicabs. These distinctive yellow vehicles with a green stripe run to set routes and the fares are fixed; pay as you get on. The destination is indicated by a sign at the front.

Trains. The Kowloon-Canton Railway (KCR) runs 21 miles (34km) from Hung Hom in Kowloon to Lo Wu and is an excellent way of visiting some of the towns and villages of the New Territories. Generally trains run every 4 to 15 minutes in each direction throughout the day. Fares are very reasonable and vary according to how far you travel.

Mass Transit Railway (MTR). The fast, air-conditioned trains of the underground railway link the central district of Hong Kong with the rest of the region. Maps in MTR stations and in every carriage depict routes, and announcements in Cantonese and English identify stops.

Purchasing MTR/KCR stored-value tickets is convenient for those using MTR frequently as it saves the bother of buying a separate ticket for each journey and also entitles you to travel on the Kowloon-Canton Railway.

Light Rail Transit (LRT). A high-speed surface rail system links the New Territory towns of Tuen Mun and Yuen Long. Trains run from 5:30am until 12:30am during the week and from 6am to midnight on Sundays and public holidays. Another LRT link connects Hong Kong island with the new Chek Lapkok airport.

Trams. Hong Kong's colourful double-decker trams provide a pleasant way to see the sights and an efficient means of travelling short distances. Slow but sure, they traverse the north coast of Hong Kong island between Kennedy Town and Shau Kei Wan. You enter through the rear doors. The exit is at the front, and you pay as you leave, dropping the exact amount into the fare box. It's a flat rate regardless of the distance travelled. The service operates between 6am and 1am.

Taxis. Hong Kong's metered taxis (with white taxi signs on the roofs) are relatively inexpensive. The law does not compel a driver to stop when hailed, even if his "for hire" flag is showing. Taxis are also not permitted to pick up (or set down) on a yellow line. But once you have successfully stopped a taxi and taken a seat, you have the legal right to be taken wherever you say.

Many drivers have a limited knowledge of English. A further problem for Westerners: places with English names normally have different ones in Chinese. So it might be useful to have someone write your destination on a piece of paper in Chinese characters. Or you can point to the location, using the maps in this book or our glossary of Hong Kong place names on page 26. Tipping is not obligatory but it's customary to add about 10 percent to the charge on the meter.

Ferries. Hundreds of thousands of passengers cross Hong Kong harbour every day on ferryboats. The boat that is most familiar to tourists is the Star Ferry, the fastest, cheapest, and most pleasant way to go between Tsimshatsui (Kowloon) and central Hong Kong. The ferries operate from 6:30am to 11:30pm. The Hong Kong Ferry

Hong Kong

(Holdings) Company serves Kowloon ports as well as outlying islands. Ferries ply regularly, from 7am to as late as midnight.

Funicular. The modernized Peak Tram funicular railway links Garden Road with Victoria Peak. The climb straight up the mountainside to the Peak Tower takes a breathtaking eight minutes; from the top there's a panoramic view of Hong Kong and, on clear days, the South China Sea. The service runs from 7am to midnight. It is a popular tourist attraction and crowded on Sundays and holidays.

Rickshaws. On a small scale they continue as a Hong Kong tourist attraction, but no new licences are issued. Fares must be agreed upon before a trip. Most tourists are content to be photographed without actually going anywhere, but this, too, requires a payment.

TRAVELLERS WITH DISABILITIES

Travellers with disabilities should contact the Hong Kong Tourist Authority (see TOURIST INFORMATION OFFICES on page 123). They will be able to provide information on accommodation and give advice on services catering for visitors with special needs. We have also indicated in our hotel listing those establishments that have special facilities or rooms specially designed for visitors with disabilities.

TRAVELLING TO HONG KONG

Consult a reliable travel agent when planning your trip.

From the United Kingdom
By air. There are several daily flights from London to Hong Kong, the majority stopping at different cities en route. Main types of fares: first class, club (business) class, economy class, excursion fare, APEX, and IPEX (Instant Purchase Excursion) fares. Flight time London-Hong Kong: 15–16 hours.

Package tours. There is a wide range of package tours available to Hong Kong with possibilities of touring in China. Most airlines offer discounts in certain Hong Kong hotels; discounts are also available on city tours.

By sea. There is no regular passenger ship between the U.K. and Hong Kong. Once or twice a year, there are round-the-world cruises leaving Europe and stopping at Hong Kong. Inquire at travel agents in your home country for further information.

From North America

By air. Scheduled flights link Hong Kong with various U.S. cities; some are direct, but most involve a stopover in either one or two cities. As well as first, business, and economy class, there are many other types of fares available between North America and Hong Kong. Prices may depend on factors such as the airline, the length of stay, the dates of travel, the date of the reservation, and the place of departure. Consult an informed travel agent well before departure. The flight time from Los Angeles to Hong Kong is approximately 17 hours; from New York, 22 hours.

Package tours. There are numerous GIT (Group Inclusive Tour) programmes for 3 to 7 days in Hong Kong and other cities in the Far East. Tour features include air transport, hotel accommodation, some or all meals, ground transport, and the services of a tour guide. These GITs may be extended by four days (but not to exceed a total of 35 days) to include trips to several cities in Asia.

There are also cruise tours with stops in Tokyo, Hong Kong, and Singapore. Or take a cruise from Singapore to Bali, then a flight home from Hong Kong.

W

WATER

Hong Kong tap water is officially qualified as safe to drink, at least when it leaves the government mains, but most local people prefer to boil it first. Bottled water is available in hotels and supermarkets. Purified ice-water is usually provided in hotel rooms and in Western-style restaurants. In Chinese restaurants the usual thirst quencher is hot tea.

a bottle of drinking water	**yat tchun sui**
iced water	**dung sui**

Hong Kong

WEIGHTS and MEASURES

Chinese measures are commonly used. Food products are generally sold by the *catty* (1.3lbs/600 g). Other items are measured by the *tael* (1.3oz/38g), and the *chin* (1.10lb/300 g). For length, the *tsün* (1.5in/37mm) and *check* (1.2ft/37cm) are used in markets.

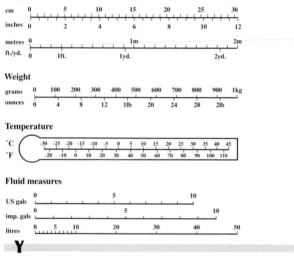

Length

| cm | 0 | 5 | 10 | 15 | 20 | 25 | 30 |
| inches | 0 | 2 | 4 | 6 | 8 | 10 | 12 |

| metres | 0 | 1m | 2m |
| ft./yd. | 0 | 1ft. | 1yd. | 2yd. |

Weight

| grams | 0 | 100 | 200 | 300 | 400 | 500 | 600 | 700 | 800 | 900 | 1kg |
| ounces | 0 | 4 | 8 | 12 | 1lb | 20 | 24 | 28 | 2lb |

Temperature

| °C | -30 -25 -20 -15 -10 -5 0 5 10 15 20 25 30 35 40 45 |
| °F | -20 -10 0 10 20 30 40 50 60 70 80 90 100 110 |

Fluid measures

US gals	0	5	10
imp. gals	0	5	10
litres	0	5	10	20	30	40	50

Y

YOUTH HOSTELS

Hong Kong's six youth hostels are located in remote scenic areas, too far to serve as a base for most foreign tourists. For information, contact the Youth Hostels Association; tel. 2788 1638.

For central accommodation there are four establishments of the YMCA and YWCA. Cheaper accommodation may be found in hostels and guest houses around town. For information, consult the Student Travel Bureau, Room 1021, Star House, Kowloon; tel. 2730 3269.

A SELECTION OF HOTELS
AND RESTAURANTS

Recommended Hotels

Hong Kong has some of the most luxurious hotels in the world, with representatives from all the major international chains. All the hotels listed are of modern design with full air-conditioning; most offer 24-hour room service and a wide range of facilities. As competition for visiting business-people is cut-throat, most Hong Kong hotels offer excellent business services and conference facilities. We have indicated those hotels which offer discounts for families sharing a room, and those with special rooms and facilities for guests with disabilities.

Reservations are strongly recommended, particularly in summer and at Christmas. If you do arrive without making advance arrangements, the Hong Kong Hotel Reservation Centre at the International Airport will be happy to arrange accommodation for you on your arrival.

As a basic guide, the symbols below have been used to indicate high-season rates per person in Hong Kong dollars, based on two people sharing a double or twin room with bath or shower. A 10% service charge and 5% government tax will be added to the bill.

✪	under $500 per person per night
✪✪	$500 to $750 per person per night
✪✪✪	over $750 per person per night

ADMIRALTY

Conrad Hotel ✪✪✪ *Pacific Place, 88 Queensway; Tel. 2521 3838; Fax 2521 3888.* Good views over the city. Cantonese, French, Italian restaurants, health centre, sauna, swimming pool, conference facilities, facilities for the disabled. 513 rooms.

Island Shangri-La Hong Kong ✪✪✪ *Pacific Place, Supreme Court Road; Tel. 2877 3838; Fax 2521 8742.* Elegant hotel furnished with abundant greenery, with Cantonese, Japanese, and Western restaurants, swimming pool, jogging track and health centre, conference facilities, and business centre. 565 rooms.

CAUSEWAY BAY

The Excelsior ✪✪✪ *281 Gloucester Road, Causeway Bay; Tel. 2894 8888; Fax 2895 6459.* Good views over the bay. Cantonese, European, and Japanese restaurants, nightclub, business centre. 888 spacious rooms.

Park Lane ✪✪✪ *310 Gloucester Road, Causeway Bay; Tel. 2890 3355; Fax 2576 7853.* Attractive, modern marble decor. American, Cantonese, and French restaurants, coffee shops, conference facilities and business centre, health centre, beauty salon. 815 rooms. Family discounts are available.

Richmond Hotel ✪✪ *1A Wang Tak Street, Happy Valley; Tel. 2574 9922; Fax 2838 1622.* Tastefully and comfortably decorated with antique-style furnishings. Banquet and conference facilities, Cantonese restaurant. 39 rooms.

CENTRAL

Hotel Furama Kempinski Hong Kong ✪✪✪ *1 Connaught Road; Tel. 2525 5111; Fax 2845 9339.* Sumptuous decor, good views, and excellent Cantonese food. French, Japanese, and international restaurants. Sauna and gym, conference facilities, and business centre. 516 rooms.

Mandarin Oriental ✪✪✪ *5 Connaught Road; Tel. 2522 0111; Fax 2810 6190.* Extravagant decor and good views over the harbour. French, Cantonese, and international restaurants; theme nights can be arranged. Conference facilities, translation service, Roman swimming pool, sauna, massage, gym, shopping centre. 541 rooms.

KOWLOON

Bangkok Royal ✪ *2-12 Pilken Street, Yau Ma Tei; Tel. 2735 9181; Fax 2730 2209.* Very reasonable rates in this small hotel just off Nathan Road. American, Cantonese, and Thai restaurants. 70 rooms.

Golden Mile Holiday Inn ✪✪✪ *50 Nathan Road, Tsimshatsui; Tel. 2369 3111; Fax 2369 8016.* American, Cantonese, and German restaurants, health centre, swimming pool, conference facilities, and business centre. 528 rooms.

Grand Stanford Harbour View Hotel ✪✪✪ *70 Mody Road, Tsimshatsui East; Tel. 2721 5161; Fax 2732 2233.* On the waterfront, with views over the harbour. French and international restaurants. Conference rooms, business centre, heated outdoor pool, sauna and gym. 592 rooms. Family discounts.

Hyatt Regency ✪✪✪ *67 Nathan Road, Kowloon; Tel. 2311 1234; Fax 2739 8701.* In a central location on Nathan Road, incorporating a three-storey shopping arcade. Comfortable and attractively furnished. Containsone of Hong Kong's finest Cantonese restaurants, a Continental restaurant and café, beauty salon, and business centre. 723 rooms. Caters to guests with disabilities.

Imperial Hotel ✪✪ *30-34 Nathan Road, Tsimshatsui; Tel. 2366 2201; Fax 2311 2360.* Coffee shop and bar, but no restaurant. 186 rooms. Family discounts.

International Hotel ✪ *33 Cameron Road, Tsimshatsui; Tel. 2366 3381; Fax 2369 5381.* Chiu Chow and French restaurants, coffee shop, and lounge. 89 rooms.

King's Hotel ✪ *473 Nathan Raod, Yau Ma Tei; Tel. 2780 1281; Fax 2782 1833.* Small hotel by Hong Kong standards, away from the main tourist area of Kowloon near the jade market. American, Cantonese, and Thai restaurants. 72 rooms.

Kowloon Hotel ✪✪✪ *19-21 Nathan Road, Tsimshatsui; Tel. 2739 9811; Fax 369 8698.* Popular tourist hotel, with Cantonese and Italian restaurants, beauty salon, and business centre. 736 rooms.

Kowloon Shangri La ✪✪✪ *64 Mody Road, Tsimshatsui; Tel. 2721 2111; Fax 2723 8686.* Elegant marble decor, relaxed atmosphere. Cantonese, French, Continental, and Japanese restaurants, swimming pool and health centre conference facilities, and business centre. Family discounts.

Hotel Nikko Hong Kong ✪✪✪ *72 Mody Road, Tsimshatsui East; Tel. 2739 1111; Fax 2311 3122.* Cantonese, French, and Japanese restaurants, coffee shop, health centre, beauty salon, and swimming pool. 442 rooms.

Nathan Hotel ✪ *378 Nathan Road, Yau Ma Tei; Tel. 2388 5141; Fax 2770 4262.* European restaurant, coffee shop, business centre. 186 rooms.

Omni Hong Kong ✪✪✪ *Harbour City, Canton Road; Tsimshatsui; Tel. 2736 0088; Fax 2736 0011.* One of a group of tourist-oriented hotels; guests can use facilities at any of the group. Cantonese, Chiu Chow, French, and Japanese restaurants, swimming pool, conference facilities, and business centre. 665 rooms.

Omni Marco Polo ✪✪✪ *Harbour City, Canton Road; Tel. 2736 0888; Fax 2736 0022.* Continental and French restaurants, business centre, and conference facilities. 437 rooms.

Omni Prince ✪✪✪ *Harbour City, Canton Road; Tel. 2736 1888; Fax 2736 0066.* Southeast Asian and international restaurants, business centre and conference facilities, swimming pool. 350 rooms.

Hong Kong

Peninsula ✪✪✪ *Salisbury Road, Kowloon; Tel. 2366 6251; Fax 2722 4170.* Hotel originally opened in 1928, in centre of Kowloon, and recently renovated and extended. Cantonese, French, Japanese, and Swiss restaurants. Well equipped, with shopping centre, business centre, private fax lines in all rooms, spa facilities, swimming pool, and sun terrace. 300 rooms. Facilities for guests with disabilities.

Regal Kowloon ✪✪ *71 Mody Road, Tsimshatsui; Tel. 2722 1818; Fax 2369 6950.* Cantonese and French restaurants, health centre, swimming pool, conference facilities, and business centre. 600 rooms. Family discounts.

Regent ✪✪✪ *18 Salisbury Road, Kowloon; Tel. 2721 1211; Fax 2739 4546.* One of Hong Kong's top hotels, set in gardens, with opulent marble decor and views of the waterfront. Sauna, outdoor swimming pool, solarium, and massage facilities, business centre, banquet suites, 7 restaurants. 602 rooms.

Royal Garden ✪✪✪ *69 Mody Road, Tsimshatsui East; Tel. 2721 5215; Fax 2369 9976.* All rooms open onto terrace over plant-filled atrium. Cantonese, European, and Italian restaurants; swimming pool, beauty salon, gym, sauna, jacuzzi, and massage facilities, conference facilities and business centre. 422 rooms.

Royal Pacific Hotel and Towers ✪ *33 Canton Road, Tsimshatsui; Tel. 2736 1188; Fax 2736 1212.* Attractive hotel surrounded by greenery, overlooking the harbour. Swiss restaurant, coffee shop, health centre, squash courts, conference facilities, beauty salon. 642 rooms.

Shamrock ✪ *223 Nathan Road, Yau Ma Tei; Kowloon; Tel. 2735 2271; Fax 2736 7354.* Stark modern building, but very reasonable rates. American and Chinese restaurants, bar, and coffee shop. 147 rooms.

Sheraton Hotel and Towers ✪✪✪ *20 Nathan Road, Kowloon; Tel. 2369 1111; Fax 2739 8707.* On the harbourfront at the corner of Nathan Road. Japanese, Cantonese, Tandoori, and international restaurants; rooftop pool and jacuzzi, sauna and gym, terrace gardens; shopping centre, conference facilities. Executive accommodation with butler service. 805 rooms. Family discounts and facilities for guests with disabilities.

Stanford Hotel Hong Kong ✪ *118 Soy Street, Mong Kok, Kowloon; Tel. 2781 1881; Fax 2388 3733.* Cantonese and international restaurants. 168 rooms.

NEW TERRITORIES

Regal Riverside ✪✪ *Tai Chung Kiu Road, Sha Tin; Tel. 2649 7878; Fax 2637 4748.* Cantonese, Thai, and international restaurants, conference facilities, and business centre. Family discounts. 828 rooms.

Royal Park ✪✪ *8 Pak Hok Ting Street, Sha Tin; Tel. 2601 2111; Fax 2601 3666.* Chiu Chow and Japanese restaurants, coffee shop, squash, tennis and jogging facilities, swimming pool, health centre, business centre, and conference facilities. Special facilities for guests with disabilities. 448 rooms.

TAI KOO

Grand Plaza ✪✪ *2 Kornhill Road, Quarry Bay, Tai Koo; Tel. 2886 0011, Fax 2886 1738.* Situated on the new residential development near Quarry Bay. Various international restaurants; health centre, swimming pool, tennis; conference facilities. 490 rooms.

WANCHAI

Century Hong Kong ✪✪ *238 Jaffe Road, Tel. 2598 8888; Fax 2598 8866.* Near the Hong Kong Convention Centre and MTR. Bars and Italian restaurants; health centre, open-air swimming pool; conference facilities, meeting rooms, and business centre. 506 rooms. Non-smoking floor and exclusive executive accommodation. Family discounts.

Hong Kong

Charterhouse Hotel ✪✪ *209-219 Wanchai Road, Wanchai; Tel. 2833 5566; Fax 2833 5888;* Continental and Cantonese restaurants, health centre, business centre. 237 rooms, including room for guests with disabilities.

Empire Hotel ✪ *33 Hennessy Road, Wanchai; Tel. 2866 9111; Fax 2861 3121.* Cantonese and international restaurants; health centre and pool; conference facilities and business centre. 341 rooms.

Grand Hyatt Hong Kong ✪✪✪ *1 Harbour Road, Wanchai; Tel. 2588 1234; Fax 2802 0677.* Futuristic design of marble and glass, with magnificent views over Hong Kong harbour. Luxurious, Art-Deco style interior. Exceptional executive accommodation with access to 24-hour butler. Business centre, reference library, private boardroom. Eight restaurants, bars, nightclub, outdoor swimming pools, gym, tennis courts, golf driving range. Special facilities for guests with disabilities. 572 rooms.

Luk Kwok Hotel ✪✪ *72 Gloucester Road, Wanchai; Tel. 2866 2166; Fax 2866 2622.* Near the Hong Kong Convention Centre in the heart of Wanchai business district, near the MTR. Spacious rooms all on high floors with superb views. Cantonese and international restaurant bar; business centre, conference rooms. 198 rooms.

New World Harbour View ✪✪✪ *1 Harbour Road, Wanchai; Tel. 2802 8888; Fax 2802 8833.* Cantonese, Continental, and international restaurants; health centre, beauty salon, tennis court, jogging track and swimming pool; conference facilities and business centre; nightclub. 790 rooms. Family discounts.

South Pacific Hotel ✪✪ *23 Morrison Hill Road, Wanchai; Tel. 2572 3838; Fax 2893 7773.* Chiu Chow restaurant, coffee shop, and conference facilities; caters to guests with disabilities. 293 rooms.

Wharney Hotel ✪✪ *57-73 Lockart Road, Wanchai; Tel. 2861 1000; Fax 2865 6023.* Cantonese and international restaurants, health centre and swimming pool, conference facilities and business centre. 332 rooms.

Recommended Restaurants

Hong Kong is crammed with all kinds and sizes of restaurants, specializing in every imaginable food from Indian and Asian cuisine to New York-style delis. Kowloon has a particularly high concentration of restaurants, of which we have only listed a limited number. We have restricted our selection to those restaurants situated in the main tourist areas, and, with a few exceptions, have not included the many excellent hotel restaurants.

Like everything in Hong Kong, the restaurants are in a constant state of flux, so the establishments listed are liable to change hands or close down at short notice. It is wise to make a table reservation before you leave your hotel.

The price symbols below are intended as a guide only, and are based on a standard three-course meal (or Asian equivalent), without alcohol, in Hong Kong dollars. The given prices do not cover luxury items such as bird's nest, truffles, caviar, or expensive seasonal seafood.

✪	up to $100 per person
✪✪	$100 to $200 per person
✪✪✪	$200 to $300 per person
✪✪✪✪	$300 and over per person

CAUSEWAY BAY

Cammino Restaurant ✪✪ *l/F, The Excelsior, 281 Gloucester Road, Causeway Bay; Tel. 2837 6780.* Appetizing menu of classic and modern Italian dishes served in friendly and relaxed atmosphere. Veal, chicken, and seafood dishes are recommended.

Hong Kong Chung Chuk Lau Restaurant ✪✪ *30 Leighton Road, Causeway Bay; Tel. 2577 4914.* Specializing in Mongolian hotpot during the winter months, when diners cook their selections in a table-top steaming pot of stock. This traditional restaurant also offers a full menu of Peking and other regional dishes.

King Heung Restaurant ✪✪✪ *G/F, Riviera Mansion, 59-65 Paterson Street; Causeway Bay; Tel. 2577 1035.* Established Peking restaurant with Peking duck and sesame shrimps on toast a house speciality.

Rangoon Restaurant ✪ *G/F, 265 Gloucester Road, Causeway Bay; Tel. 2893 2281;* Cheerful café serving spicy Burmese dishes — mild curries, spiced soups, and rice and noodle dishes.

Sui Sha Ya Japanese Restaurant ✪✪✪✪ *1/F, Lockhart House, 440 Jaffe Road, Causeway Bay; Tel. 2838 1808.* Sushi, *sashimi*, and *tempura* dishes are served in traditional Japanese decor. Service is friendly.

Vegi Food Kitchen ✪✪ *Highland Mansion, 8 Cleveland Street, Causeway Bay; Tel. 2890 6603.* Serves imaginative and tasty vegetarian dishes, attractively presented. A small but elegant restaurant. No meat or alcohol may be brought onto the premises.

CENTRAL

Ashoka Restaurant ✪ *G/F, 57-59 Wyndham Street, Central; Tel. 2524 9623.* Elegant Indian restaurant serving *à la carte* and set meals of delicately spiced Mogul cuisine. The wide range of dishes offered includes Tandoori dishes, curries, kormas, and vegetarian specialities.

Beirut ✪✪ *G/F-1/F, 27 D'Aguilar Street, Lan Kwai Fong, Central; Tel. 2804 6611.* Newly-opened restaurant serving an extensive menu of Lebanese specialities, including Shawarma and sandwiches. The home-made humous is the best in Hong Kong. Ideal for lunch.

Benkay Japanese Restaurant ✪✪✪ *1st Basement, Gloucester Tower, The Landmark; 11 Pedder Street, Central; Tel. 2808 0608.* Elegant pine-panelled restaurant serving *teppanyaki* and *sushi* delicacies, or *sukiyaki* or *shabu-shabu* set meals. The *à la carte* menu features Kyoto-style cuisine; the grilled codfish and eel are particularly recommended.

Bentley's Seafood Restaurant Oyster Bar ✪✪✪ *B4, Basement, Prince's Building, 10 Chater Road, Central; Tel. 2868 0881.* This English-style seafood restaurant is a branch of the famous London parent, and serves similar high-quality seafood specialities. Cocktail bar and oyster bar.

Brasserie on the Eighth ✪✪✪ *Hotel Conrad, Pacific Place, 88 Queensway, Central; Tel. 2521 3838.* Menu of hearty, traditional French specialities. A variety of fresh seafood and grilled meats is also available.

La Bodega ✪✪ *G/F, 31 Wyndham Street; Tel. 2877 5472.* Spanish-style restaurant serving a wide range of dishes from tapas-bar snacks to the full traditional *paella*. Recently renovated. The atmosphere is relaxed and the service friendly.

California ✪✪ *G/F, Grand Progress Building, 15 Lan Kwai Fong, Central; Tel. 2521 1345.* American-style restaurant and bar popular with the after-work crowd from Central. Several "California" favourites are offered such as vegetarian foccaccia sandwiches, fajitas, and (of course) a vast selection of hamburgers.

Chiu Chow Garden Restaurant ✪ *G/F, Lippo Centre, Queensway, Central; Tel. 2845 1323.* A popular Chiu Chow restaurant. Particular specialities are peanut puffs, and the freshwater "ricefish" hotpot.

Fortuna Yakitori Store Ltd ✪✪ *6/f, Cota Plaza, 51 Garden Road; Tel. 2523 3030.* Bistro-style Japanese restaurant serving a wide range of seafood *sushi*, *sashimi*, and *robatayaki* snacks. Fresh lobster a speciality.

Nanbantei Yakitori Restaurant ✪✪✪ *G/F, Bank of America Tower, Shop 7a, 12 Harcourt Road, Central; Tel. 2526 7678.* Yakitori (charcoal-grilled herbed chicken) and other snacks served on small wooden skewers, such as bacon-wrapped salmon, garlic-spiced meats, scallops, and pork-wrapped asparagus.

Peking Garden Restaurant ✪✪ *Shop 003, The Mall, Pacific Place, 88 Queensway, Central; Tel. 2845 8452.* Lively restaurant specializing in spectacular northern Chinese and Peking dishes. Watch fresh noodles being made each evening, and enjoy the Peking duck-carving exhibitions and beggar's chicken clay-breaking ceremonies.

Pierrot Restaurant ✪✪✪✪ *Mandarin Oriental, 5 Connaught Road, Central; Tel. 2522 0111.* Fine French cuisine is served in this exclusive hotel restaurant, which boasts Asia's only caviar restaurant. Dramatic views down over the bay; private dining room available.

Shanghai Garden Restaurant ✪✪ *Hutchison House, 10 Harcourt Road, Central; Tel. 2524 8181.* Sophisticated restaurant specializing in the cuisine of China's eastern region, with cocktail lounge and upstairs restaurant. Provincial specialities also include a range of classic dishes from various other regions of China.

Supatra's ✪✪ *G/F, 50 D'Aguilar Street, Lan Kwai Fong. Central; Tel. 2522 5073.* This cheerful Thai restaurant and bar offers a wide variety of delicious spicy dishes. The traditional *tam yam kung* soup and garlic king prawns are a must.

KOWLOON

Bodhi Vegetarian Restaurant ✪✪ *2/F, 81 Nathan Road, Tsimshatsui; Tel. 2739 2222.* Attractive presentation of a wide variety of Chinese vegetarian dishes and "soul-cleansing" dishes; no alcohol is allowed on the premises. Specialities include beancurd, mushrooms, and bamboo-shoot dishes.

City Chiu Chow Restaurant ✪✪ *1/F, East Ocean Centre, 98 Granville Road, Tsimshatsui; Tel. 2723 6226.* Bright and comfortable restaurant serving typical hearty Chiu Chow dishes and a variety of regional specialities. More strongly flavoured than Cantonese food.

East Ocean Seafood Restaurant ✪✪ *B-l, East Ocean Centre, 98 Granville Road, Tsimshatsui East; Tel. 2723 8128.* Good-quality, inexpensive seafood. Set meals are particularly good value. Despite the name the regular menu features pigeon and venison as well as a range of seafood dishes.

Fook Lam Moon Restaurant ✪✪✪✪ *Shop 8, l/F, 53-59 Kimberley Road, Tsimshatsui; Tel. 2366 0286.* A well-known Cantonese restaurant specializing in seafood; the "pan-fried lobster balls" are an experience not to be missed.

Golden Island Bird's Nest Chiu Chow Restaurant ✪✪ *3/F-4/F, BCC Building, 25-31 Carnarvon Road, Tsimshatsui; Tel. 2369 5211.* A good restaurant for the health-conscious, serving non-oily, low-cholesterol Chiu Chow dishes. Particularly recommended are the soyed goose and bird's nest.

Great Shanghai Restaurant ✪ *26 Prat Avenue, Tsimshatsui; Tel. 2366 8158.* Well-established restaurant serving good-value Shanghainese dishes. Try some of the typical warming dishes such as Shanghainese dumplings, eel and beancurd dishes, and cabbage stews. Shanghainese wines are also available. Friendly and helpful service.

Harbour View Seafood Restaurant ✪ *3/F, Tsimshatsui Centre, West Wing, 66 Mody Road, Tsimshatsui East; Tel. 2722 5888.* Spacious restaurant with magnificent views of the harbour. Try the *dim sum*, especially the delicious shrimp and scallop dumplings.

Heichinrou Restaurant ✪✪✪ *2/F, Lippo Sun Plaza, 28 Canton Road, Tsimshatsui; Tel. 2375 7123.* A chic Cantonese restaurant with stark modern decor. Specialities include roasted pigeon with Chinese cheese sauce, and Spanish noodles. The lunchtime *dim sum* are particularly good.

Jade Garden Restaurant ✪✪ *BCC Bank Building, 25-31 Carnarvon Road, Tsimshatsui; Tel. 2369 8311.* Classic dishes and seasonal specialities, including double-boiled duck with parsley and pan-fried stuffed beancurd. Ask for the recommended dishes of the day.

Jade Terrace Restaurant ✪✪✪ *2/F, Peninsula Centre; 67 Mody Road, Tsimshatsui East; Tel. 2311 8888.* Modern Cantonese restaurant with marble and glass decor. Advance orders taken for abalone, bird's nest, pigeon, and chicken specialities. Other specialities include baked stuffed scallops. Also features karaoke facilities.

Java Rijsttafel Restaurant ✪ *G/F, Han Hing Mansion, 38 Hankow Road, Tsimshatsui; Tel. 2367 1230.* A small and friendly bistro-style restaurant serving authentic Indonesian meals and snacks. Menu of satay, Malay curries, *gado-gado,* and desserts. Reservations are recommended.

Lai Ching Heen ✪✪✪✪ *Regent Hotel, 18 Salisbury Road, Tsimshatsui; Tel. 2721 1211.* Elegant Cantonese restaurant with opulent decor and views over the harbour. *A la carte* menu of luxury dishes; monthly specialities.

Maharaja II ✪ *G/F, 1-3A Granville Circuit , Tsimshatsui; Tel. 2366 6671.* Good-value Indian restaurant, serving a wide range of dishes, including biryanis, classic Moghlai meat and vegetarian dishes, Tandoori kebabs, and fresh breads.

North China Peking Seafood Restaurant ✪ *2/F-3/F, Poly Commercial Building, 21-23 Prat Avenue, Tsimshatsui; Tel. 2311 6689.* Friendly, relaxed restaurant serving delicious Peking duck, home-made noodles, onion cakes, and dumplings.

Orchard Court Restaurant ✪✪ *1/F-2/F, Ma's Mansion, 37 Hankow Road, Tsimshatsui; Tel. 2317 5111.* Showcase fish tanks add interest to this elegant restaurant. Traditional and modern dishes include BBQ Peking duck, baked stuffed whelk, "drunken" shrimps flambée, and sautéed minced pigeon.

Shanghai Restaurant ✪✪ *G/F, 24 Prat Avenue, Tsimshatsui; Tel. 2739 7083.* Typical Shanghainese dishes and more unusual specialities, such as Yellow River fish, steamed buns, and Tientsin cabbage with shrimps. Small portions are ideal for sampling a range of dishes.

Tai Woo Restaurant ✪ *14-16 Hillwood Road, Tsimshatsui; Tel. 2369 9773.* Popular favourites include seafood dishes such as steamed garoupa or sautéed scallops. The set meals are a good way of sampling a range of Cantonese dishes.

Tien Heung Lau Restaurant ✪✪ *G/F, 18C Austin Avenue, Tsimshatsui, Tel. 2368 9660.* Small, old-fashioned restaurant which serves Hangzhou specialities. This restaurant concentrates on top-quality food rather than smart decor, and the furnishings are simple. Look for classic West Lake dishes, and order in advance for beggar's chicken.

THE PEAK

Café Deco ✪✪✪ *1/F-2/F Peak Galleria, 118 Peak Road, The Peak; Tel. 2849 5111.* A recent addition to Hong Kong, boasting one of the best views in the city. In addition to a variety of Asian and Continental dishes, Café Deco offers an oyster bar and live jazz on the weekends.

Peak Café ✪✪ *121 Peak Road, The Peak ; Tel. 2819 5111.* This café has become a Hong Kong institution. Situated in a 19th-century building at the top of Victoria Peak, it has old-world charm as well as stunning views over the south side of the island. Ideal for lunch or tea after a ride up on the tram from Central.

WANCHAI

Can Do Restaurant ✪ *1/F, 78 Johnston Road, Tsimshatsui, Wanchai; Tel. 2527 7868.* Specialities include sweet-and-sour *won ton* and special *congees*. Serves good-value snacks and meals, and service is friendly. A popular restaurant with both visitors and local residents.

Cinta Restaurant ✪✪ *1/F-2/F, Shing Yip Building, 10 Fenwick Street, Wanchai; Tel. 2527 1199.* Multi-ethnic restaurant serving Indonesian favourites such as satay, prawn chilli, fried squid, and beef Rendang. Filipino dishes include crispy *pata* (pork leg) and mixed *adobo*. Live entertainment.

American Restaurant ✪ *G/F-2/F, 20 Lockhart Road, Wanchai; Tel. 2527 1000.* Popular Peking restaurant (despite the puzzling name) featuring northern Chinese dishes of warming food, such as seafood noodles and the classic Peking duck. House favourite is a "Four Great Happiness" combination dish of pork, beef, prawns, and chicken.

Swatow Garden Restaurant ✪✪ *Basement 1, South Pacific Hotel, 23 Morrison Hill Road, Wanchai; Tel. 2572 3838 ext. 1388.* Set meals are particularly good value. Unusual specialities include braised eggplant and minced pork with spicy sauce, and pan-fried oyster omelette.

Viceroy of India ✪✪ *2/F, Sun Hung Kai Centre, 30 Harbour Road, Wanchai; Tel. 2827 7777.* Indian restaurant with panoramic harbour views and outdoor terrace, serving subtly flavoured Tandoori, curry, and vegetarian specialities, and an all-you-can-eat weekday buffet feast.